PARIS BY NIGHT

Frommer's

PARIS
by Night

BY

ALEXANDER F. LOBRANO

A BALLIETT & FITZGERALD BOOK

MACMILLAN • USA

a disclaimer

Prices fluctuate in the course of time, and travel information changes under the impact of the varied and volatile factors that influence the travel industry. Neither the author nor the publisher can be held responsible for the experiences of readers while traveling. Readers are invited to write to the publisher with ideas, comments, and suggestions for future editions.

about the author

Alexander F. Lobrano, a confirmed noctambule, is a food, travel, and style writer based in Paris, where he has lived for nine years. He is the European Contributing Editor for *Departures* magazine and writes for a variety of other magazines and newspapers, including the *International Herald Tribune,* the *Los Angeles Times, Travel & Leisure, Food & Wine,* and *Town & Country.* He is currently working on a novel.

Balliett & Fitzgerald, Inc.
Executive editor: Tom Dyja
Managing editor: Duncan Bock
Editor: Laura Kelly
Associate editor: Howard Slatkin
Assistant editor: Maria Fernandez
Editorial assistant: Brooke Holmes
Special thanks to Judy Fayard.

Macmillan Travel art director: Michele Laseau

All maps © Simon & Schuster, Inc.

MACMILLAN TRAVEL
A Simon & Schuster Macmillan Company
1633 Broadway
New York, NY 10019

ISBN 0-02-861128-4
ISSN 1088-470X

special sales

Bulk purchases (10+ copies) of Frommer's Travel Guides are available to corporations at special discounts. The Special Sales Department can produce custom editions to be used as premiums and/or for sales promotions to suit individual needs. Existing editions can be produced with custom cover imprints such as corporate logos. For more information write to: Special Sales, Simon & Schuster, 1633 Broadway, New York, NY 10019.

Manufactured in the United States of America

contents

Paris Orientation

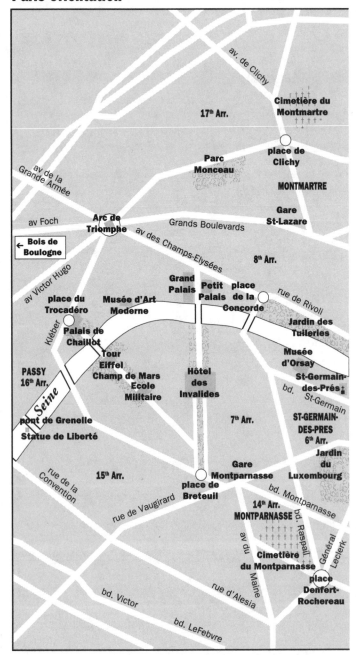

av. de Clichy

Cimetière du Montmartre

17ᵗʰ Arr.

place de Clichy

Parc Monceau

MONTMARTRE

av de la Grande Armée

Gare St-Lazare

av Foch

Arc de Triomphe

Grands Boulevards

av des Champs-Elysées

← **Bois de Boulogne**

8ᵗʰ Arr.

av Victor Hugo

Grand Palais

Petit Palais

place de la Concorde

rue de Rivoli

place du Trocadéro

Musée d'Art Moderne

Jardin des Tuileries

Kléber

Palais de Chaillot

Musée d'Orsay

Tour Eiffel

St-Germain-des-Prés

PASSY 16ᵗʰ Arr.

Champ de Mars Ecole Militaire

Hôtel des Invalides

bd. St-Germain

Seine

ST-GERMAIN-DES-PRES 6ᵗʰ Arr.

pont de Grenelle

Statue de Liberté

7ᵗʰ Arr.

Jardin du Luxembourg

rue de la Convention

15ᵗʰ Arr.

Gare Montparnasse

place de Breteuil

bd. Montparnasse

rue de Vaugirard

14ᵗʰ Arr.

MONTPARNASSE

bd. Raspail

av du Maine

Cimetière du Montparnasse

Général Leclerc

place Denfert-Rochereau

bd. Victor

rue d'Alesia

bd. LeFebvre

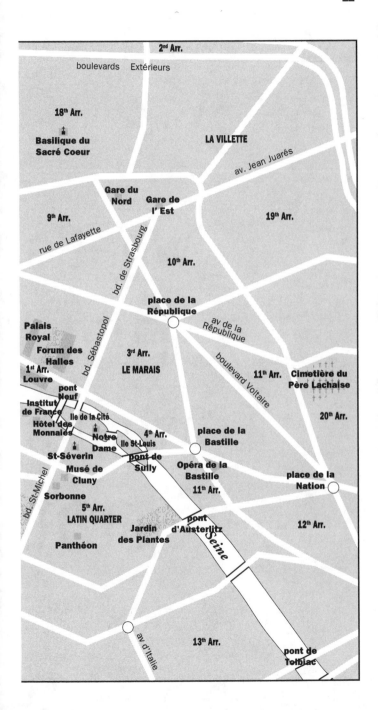

what's
hot,
what's
not

Paris is the most beautiful city in the world, but it's also moody, snobbish, and expensive. Once you know this, your fail-safe irony will see you through otherwise maddening encounters with its occasionally fussy ways. The best approach, really, to playing in Paris after dark is not to adopt the usual North American colonial crouch before people, places, and situations you don't know or immediately understand. A lot of confidence and a little arrogance will work wonders. So be polite, but don't be cowed, and hey, how would you know that the French absolutely never drink coffee with milk after a meal unless you'd been here before?

Almost as much as Los Angeles and Miami, Paris is a city where appearance is everything. This might ruffle your PC sensibilities, but when in Rome.... So suffice it to say that if you're looking fabulous, you're going to have a lot more fun and a much easier time of things than if you stick to the standard tourist's costume of T-shirt, jeans, and jogging shoes. Coming from super-casual North America, you might even find a little elegance bracing, for that matter.

Depending upon your agenda, there are certain Parisian experiences you've just *got* to have. Take in one of the big boom-boom discos, like **Le Palace** or **Les Bains**, or if you're gay or with gay friends, **Le Queen**, and then go eat a tray of oysters at **Au Pied de Cochon** or a huge steak at **La Tour de Montlhery**, both in Les Halles. Don your Commes des Garçons and see whatever's going on at the **Opéra Garnier**, the mother of all opera houses, and then head over to the **What's Up Bar**, near the Bastille, to toss back a drink or two with the fashionable regulars. Downshift some other night and do all of the sepia-toned stuff, like an excursion on the Seine in one of **Les Vedettes de Pont Neuf**: You can put up with ninety minutes of feeling a bit like a tourist turkey for something this beautiful. Then have a salad at the **Café de Flore** in Saint-Germain-des-Prés (they're really expensive but good), before taking in the late show at **La Pagode Cinéma**, and then having a nightcap at **Le Birdland** or heading over to the **New Morning** for some jazz. Whatever itinerary you may plot, some night you have to walk back to your hotel, since the ultimate pleasure of Paris after dark is Paris.

What's hot

Club-restaurant-bars... Le Reservoir, the wildly hot new club-restaurant-bar near the Bastille, is typical of the hybrid places that are becoming popular as one-stop entertainment. In a wonderfully foolish mock-medieval atmosphere, you can dine while listening to jazz, soul, or Latino singers. The crowd catches the tip of the wave between 25 and 35 and is an appealing mix of artists, media people, architects, designers, advertising folks, art directors, and other creative types. French yuppies are known as *BCBG*s *(Bon Chic, Bon Gens)*, a very *au courant* local term with an appropriate whiff of snobbery because it denotes upper-middle-class professionals with aristocratic pretentions. The *BCBG*s have made **Barfly**, a restaurant-bar in the eighth arrondissement's George V hotel, another recent hit. Among their other favorite watering holes—and this crowd's not shy around a bottle—are **L'Arc**, **Les Bains**, **Castel's Princess**, and when adventurous, the **China Club**. The fashion crowd (an international herd of models, publicists, designers, photographers, and journalists, often dressed in black and vexingly prone to wearing sunglasses indoors) migrates around town according to the latest word from their own grapevine. But this group is usually much in evidence at the **Cafe Marly** at the Louvre, bars like **Stolly's** and **Chez Richard**, the restaurant **Chez Omar** in the Marais, and a bouquet of clubs ranging from their essential mainstay, **Les Bains**, to **Le Queen**, the **Bataclan**, and the odd one-nighter at **Le Palace**, the grand dame of Paris discos, currently enjoying a new lease on life since new management took over from fading club queen Régine.

Bars with deejays... The deejay bars sprouting up in Paris's major *quartier de nuit* are perfect pre-club or great nights out on their own. The ultimate deejay bar is the **What's Up Bar** near the Bastille, where star spinners like Laurent Garnier and musicians like M.C. Solaar will make your body move. Also around the Bastille is the truly hip **Bar des Ferailleurs**, while the funky, friendly world music of **Le Satellit Café** isn't far away. **Le Comptoir** and the **Angel Café** in Les Halles, and **Club Club** in Pigalle, are also hot on this circuit. One only wishes that the deejays in the big clubs were as good as those found in these bars.

Cocktails... Whether it's Catherine Deneuve sipping a bourbon sour in **Le Belier**, the bar in the hotel L'Hôtel, or hot young designer Veronique Leroy grooving over a martini at **Le Satellit Café**, Parisians are into cocktails these days. Margaritas reign supreme, even if they're not usually very good anywhere but at **La Perla** or **Chez Richard**, both in the Marais. In search of the ultimate Bloody Mary, the crowd's getting younger at the venerable **Harry's Bar**, while martini lovers should treat themselves to the **Hemingway Bar** at the Ritz, or, more fun, the **China Club**. If you'd throw yourself into the Seine unless you could get such American-style party fuel as a Long Island Iced Tea, try **The Lizard Lounge** in the Marais. (See The Bar Scene.)

Wild & Lethal Trash... Though you may have been so described by your friends, what's being referred to here is the hottest clubgear label in Europe, especially if you're into techno or trance music. Think a lemon yellow pile vest with red faux-crocodile sleeves. These groovy duds are the product of the winningly febrile imagination of Belgian designer Walter Van Bierendonck. The shoes to match come from **Freelance**, an off-the-wall French shoe label. More decorous types cobble their club look together at **A.P.C.**, French designer Jean Toitou's label, which has a very understated Saint-Germain-in-the-fifties minimalist chic.

Nightlife shows on television... The best of the three or four new and popular television shows about Paris at night is media magnate Thierry Ardisson's "**Paris Dernier**," which runs every Saturday at 11:30pm on the cable channel Paris Première. Ardisson, a bit of a naughty playboy, takes you along as he meets friends like Gina Lollobrigida for a drink, checks out an unnamed and dubiously authentic lesbian S&M club, drops by Castel's Princess for a turn on the floor to some Bee Gees music, and so on.

Cigars... Stogies are the stylish way to create a smoke screen in Paris, where people are still relatively relaxed about things—tobacco amongst them. There's even a successful new restaurant, **La Casa de Habano**, that caters to cigar lovers with an excellent climate-controlled cigar boutique on the premises. For those who don't smoke cigars, it comes equipped with a state-of-the-art ventilation system. The **China Club** also offers a first-rate assortment of Cuban beauties.

Laurent Garnier... Former star of the Hacienda Club in Manchester, England, Laurent brought true British club culture back to Paris with him, and real party people just can't get enough. He's currently installed at the **Rex Club**, but often hosts special nights elsewhere and likes to hang out at the **What's Up Bar** in the Bastille. Laurent's best efforts notwithstanding, the Paris club scene is pretty tepid compared to London or New York.

Bistro annexes and New Wave bistros... The bistro-annex trend started about ten years ago, when haute cuisine chef Michel Rostang opened **La Bistrot d'à Côte**, an affordable bistro annex to his very expensive eponymous restaurant. It was a huge success, and now it's the rare top Paris chef who doesn't have a satellite, or, in the case of bistro-meister Guy Savoy, five. Act Two is the New Wave bistros, or very simple places, usually with a prix-fixe menu, that have been opened by a new generation of young chefs, many of whom have trained in some of the capital's grandest kitchens. (See Late Night Dining.)

Scooters... Ever since the Métro strike that paralyzed the city for a month in late 1995, Parisians of all ages have taken to motor scooters with a vengeance, and many tables in clubs and restaurants are surrounded by a ring of the *Bladerunner*-style helmets that must be worn here by law. What's made everyone double back to what was previously seen as adolescent transport is that they cost almost nothing, can be parked almost anywhere, and thread through traffic jams with ease. They also use very little gas and liberate dogged party people from taxi anxiety, especially during the weekend. With their streamlined motorcycle styling and metallic colors, Peugot makes the scooters of choice. See Down and Dirty for how to rent one.

What's not

Drag queens... Once they were a thrill, now they're just shrill. Paris clubgoers think drag's a drag. The only exception is the professional *La Cage Aux Folles*-style queens who work at clubs like **Chez Michou**; these gals really know how to wield a compact, and make RuPaul look like Martha Stewart by comparison.

Supermodels... With the exception of aristocratic Italian homegirl Carla Bruni, Parisians, always wary of hype, have had their firsthand fill of supermodels. The thinking goes that no one's worth that much money, and that we end up paying their salaries indirectly anyway. If you haven't had your dose, they hang around the disco **Les Bains**, the **What's Up Bar** and **Barfly**. Many of the males of the species are to be found at **Le Queen**.

Cultural protectionism... Everyone agrees that the new law forcing radio stations to devote at least 40 percent of their playtime to French music, of which a certain percent must be new, is a major drag. The reason behind this legislation? Protecting the French language, *bien sûr*. Similar legislation is also designed to restrict non-European— gee, what could that mean?—television programming to a minimum, and French filmmakers whine ceaselessly about the popularity of American films, which they see as evidence of cultural imperialism. National grandstanding in the age of the Internet seems pretty futile, but the French insist on putting it to the test, to the derision of many young Parisians.

Régine and her club... The proverbial queen of the Paris night recently grabbed headlines alleging an expensive tantrum aloft. Her apparent unwillingness to accept the "no smoking in the aisles" prohibition reportedly forced a Paris-Miami flight to land in Boston, where she was fined nearly a hundred thousand dollars. Making matters worse, she made a mess of Le Palace when she owned it, and her namesake club has become so tacky that it didn't make this guide.

American rap music... All the rage in Paris a few years ago, the French now prefer, frequently with good reason, the mellower sound of their own rappers. The best groups, like Ethnique Alliance from Marseilles, pride themselves on their lyrics, and their sound is much influenced by North African music. Snoop Doggy Dog and Coolio just don't make much sense in a city as smugly bourgeois as Paris.

the clu

b scene

Paris stumbled through the eighties with a seventies hangover; the European party destination par excellence during the disco years, the city never really got over the Village People.

But the end of the most recent French recession and the influence of London raves and house music has set the Paris club scene in motion again. New club venues open rarely, but a lot of the existing clubs have revised their beat for the nineties, and late-night bars like the funky **Lili la Tigresse** near the Place Pigalle offer a lively alternative to traditional discos. The other major influence on the Parisian night right now is ethnic—France has a thriving rap scene, with stars like M.C. Solaar, and is also the world capital of African music and a major center of North African music, including Algerian *rai*.

A funkier, often ethnic, and sometimes less expensive club scene with echoes of New York's Lower East Side or London's Camden Town exists around **La Bastille,** and continues to emerge in the **11th arrondisement,** one of the few parts of Paris where it's still possible to find a semi-affordable apartment. These clubs are less finicky at the door than the more expensive, big discos, and draw intriguing, mixed crowds. **La Chapelle des Lombards** and **Le Balajo,** on the **rue de Lappe** party strip, are the granddaddies of this scene, but **Le Satellit Café** (see The Bar Scene) is the most happening stop on this circuit right now, with a spicy mix of world music ranging from salsa to get-your-butt-out-of-that-chair *malagache,* a Creole music from the Indian Ocean island of Réunion.

Gays are at the head of the pack of the hard-core party crowd, and local fans of house music in a city where Euro-techno remains a menace don't have much choice beyond **Le Queen, Le Bataclan,** or the ultra-hip, ultra-exclusive, after-hours club **Le Privilège,** depending on who's spinning that evening. Note, though, that gay and straight Paris mix easily, depending, of course, on your look and attitude at the door. A good example of ambisexual Paris is the popularity of the **Banana Café** in **Les Halles,** a crowded cafe-bar with drag queens dancing on the tables and bar. This place was originally only gay, but has since gained a following of hip, young, suburban couples, especially on the weekends.

The *guingettes,* or floating barges, are another decidedly French alternative because there's no age consideration at these places—everyone from your grandmother to your little sister can get down to the range of music played in these places. This is not to say, however, that you won't see some fine dancing on the *guingettes.* Many people go just to watch the couples who've been seriously dancing together for years.

Getting Past the Velvet Rope

When the Eiffel Tower, looming over Paris in the night, is unplugged—at midnight in winter, 1am in the summer—it's the signal to Paris clubgoers that it's party time. In a city that is almost fetishistically concerned with appearances, it would not do to ring the bell or brave the velvet ropes before 1am, of course, with 1:20am being just about as calibratedly cool an hour as possible to first show face.

Just getting your timing right is only step one, though, if you seriously want to sample some of the French capital's clubs. For starters, you're going to need a lot of money; cover charges are stiff, averaging around 100 francs. Drinks tend to be very pricey; at the wildly popular gay club **Le Queen** on the Champs-Elysées, for example, a beer will cost you $15. Then, most crucially, there's the matter of how you look. Paris nightlife is very tribal, and your sartorial gaffes will be forgiven only if you're a stark raving beauty or show up on the arm of someone like Keanu Reeves or Claudia Schiffer. As a general guideline, black rules, but this does not apply to sweatshirts, stonewashed jeans, or any kind of athletic footwear. This is, after all, the fashion capital of the world. If you wore the ideal outfit for the über-yuppie, neo-aristocratic **L'Arc Club** near the Arc de Triomphe—a little black minidress and a choker with a cross or a blazer with gray flannel slacks and J. M. Weston loafers—to **Le Bataclan**, probably the hottest club in town right now, you'd guarantee yourself a place on the sidewalk out front for as long as it would take you to get the message. Before you step out, decide which of the nocturnal tribes you belong to and go chameleon, because not only your Topsiders, but the grunge, hip-hop, or Rollerblade looks aren't going to work in the City of Lights. Even when they try to be funky, Parisians just can't suppress their instinctive chic.

The Lowdown

Disco dancing... Though they may often look as if they're moving in response to extraterrestrial signals, Parisians love to dance. Discotheque is, after all, a French word, and the originals, in and around Saint-Germain-des-Prés on the Left Bank and in Saint Tropez on the Côte d'Azur, first became popular in the heyday of Brigitte Bardot. Depending on where they go, clubgoers from other cities with vital dance scenes may occasionally have the impression that the clock stopped in either 1967 or, more often the case, 1978. Perhaps reflecting the generally conservative outlook of their clientele, many of the BCBG (*Bon Chic, Bon Gens*) clubs, such as **L'Arc** and **Niel's**, both near the Arc de Triomphe, play a lot of American seventies gold, running to Gloria Gaynor and the Ritchie Family. This isn't necessarily a disaster, especially if you haven't heard "Fly Robin, Fly" for a long time, and it's generally preferable to French disco music, which is an oxymoron.

Techno music clubs... The problem the French have with rhythm might also explain the enormous popularity of techno music in Paris; everyone looks spastic when they're dancing to techno. It first started out in gay clubs, but has since gone mainstream, and many of the big discos that attract a suburban crowd on the weekends, particularly Le Rex Club north of Les Halles and **La Scala** on the rue de Rivoli, play predominantly techno. Note, too, that techno is almost inevitable in the discotheques of French provincial cities. The enormous **Rex Club** is techno heaven, especially on the nights that Laurent Garnier, the hottest deejay in Paris, spins the techno-trance mixes that drove them crazy when he was working at various clubs across the Channel in Manchester. You might find the psychedelic decor a bit hokey, but it works just fine for the crowd.

It's only rock 'n' roll... You want to go dancing but can't stand techno and think house music is a drag. Well, Paris doesn't offer a very large choice of alternatives, but there is **Le Gibus**, long one of the premier rock and heavy-metal clubs in Paris. Though it has now moved into tech-no music, this club occasionally reverts to its rock roots. It has an ambience that recalls a girls' dressing room from a 1930s dance review. The **Bus Palladium**, with its endear-ingly odd seventies decor, is the best dance venue for peo-ple who don't like any form of discotheque music. The club plays a mixture of rock standards in the Rolling Stones, Rod Stewart, Bruce Springsteen mode.

All that jazz... Since World War II, when Saint-Germain-des-Prés emerged as the buzzy hub of nightlife in post-war Paris, jazz has been associated with the Left Bank. Today, the jazz club **Le Bar** in the Hôtel Villa, a pleasant, contemporary basement space with good music, is just about the only serious jazz club left in this neighborhood. The **Bilboquet** and Latitudes, on the rue Saint-Benoit, have become tired tourist holes, but the jazz tradition sol-diers on elsewhere. The **Le Caveau de la Huchette**, a warm, student-filled place in the Latin Quarter, still offers superb shows by stars like Harry Edison, Billie Holiday's trumpeter of choice. The two **Petit Journal** venues in the Latin Quarter and Montparnasse aren't ter-ribly appealing in terms of their surroundings, but are worth braving if you really need a live jazz fix. If you want jazz in the background while you're having a late supper, **L'Arbuci** on the rue de Buci just off boulevard Saint-Germain is a late-night brasserie that offers a good, cheap, all-you-can-eat rotisserie menu and has a pleasant jazz club in the basement downstairs. The two hottest clubs in town are the famous **New Morning**, where Chet Baker was once the resident musician and where world-class talent still plays, and the up-and-coming **Hot Brass**, which showcases players like James Carter and Kenny Garrett and is extremely popular despite its inconvenient location on the northeastern edge of town. **Au Duc des Lombards**, with murals of Duke Ellington and John Coltrane on its facade, has long been one of the fabled jazz clubs of Paris, but many people have recently found its programming rather disappointing; most of the players here these days are French. Your best bet is to catch one of the Tuesday jam sessions, because it becomes unpleasantly crowded on the weekends. Other good Right Bank venues include the **Lionel Hampton Jazz Club**. It's incongruously located in a Meridien Hotel at the Porte Maillot, but is a very important jazz space that also showcases gospel, soul, and R&B. **Le Slow Club**, in the heart of town near the Louvre, attracts a fun, younger crowd; and **Le Petit Opportun**, a wonderful, medieval cellar near Les Halles, attracts a friendly crowd and often showcases emerging talent. **Le Sunset** is another good spot for serious jazz fiends.

Can-can if you must must... If the chance to peer up a lady's skirts was once a reason alone to come to Paris, the erotic promise of girlie shows has been completely eclipsed by changing mores. When you can dial into a local telephone network for rubber fetishists, viewing bare breasts seems strikingly wholesome. The production values of a lot of the big shows are downright hokey to anyone who's been to Vegas or Atlantic City, and there's something generally frigid about the whole experience. If you really want to do this, though, your best bet is **Le Moulin Rouge**, which is so ludicrous it can actually be fun. From the red, neon sign that sits atop a windmill flailing the Montmartre darkness to the audience of Bulgarian electrical engineers, dour provincial couples, and busloads of Asians, this place is pure camp. They still do a can-can number, of course, but the best part of the show is the tank of live crocodiles lowered onto the stage—their tamer is dressed like an extra from *Spartacus*. LaToya Jackson, alas, is no longer in the show, but if you like to look at half-nude girls in 50-pound sequin-and-rhinestone headdresses, and boys in glittery, Spandex bodysuits, this is the place. For something a little stiffer, if you will, try **Le Lido**, which is more upmarket and renowned in certain circles for its Bluebell Girls, all 60 of them, who shake and shimmy to the delight of a predominantly male crowd. Whatever you do, don't dine in one of these places—the food's horrendous and very expensive; just book the show. Paris also has a *La Cage aux Folles* tradition, and the best place to dally in this world of gender make-believe is **Chez Michou**, a rather hilarious place near the Place Pigalle. The "girls" here are to be admired for their reasonably convincing *trompe l'oeil*, and the show includes enough shreds of English to be amusing for non-French speakers, too.

For the college crowd... For reasons of both style (students often think discos are, as the Brits would say, naff) and economy (clubs are expensive), students in Paris generally prefer to hang out in bars and cafes. When they do decide to get down, they go to places like **Le Saint**, a friendly club in a honeycomb of 13th-century cellars in the Latin Quarter. This club is not for the claustrophobic, but offers a relatively affordable good time and music that runs from acid jazz to techno, with the odd dose of Latin or African. Almost anyone under 30 will be comfortable here, but if you're looking for something glamorous or frisky, you can do better elsewhere.

Sweet sixteen... **La Scala**, an enormous post-pubescent pleasure pit with eight bars, videos, and light shows, is the disco *par excellence* for club puppies who're just cutting their teeth. Both soldiers and *au pair* girls make a beeline for this place the moment they're let off the leash, and the club attracts a surprisingly international crowd, with many Euro-boppers elated at having ditched their parents and sightseeing duties for an evening. Unless you're nursing a Lolita complex, it's unlikely that you'd enjoy this place much if you're more than 25 years old. A far more decorous teenage fiesta occurs every Sunday afternoon at **Niel's**, the *BCBG* club near the Arc de Triomphe. Called Le P'tit Niel's, it's lunch with entertainment and dancing for 4- to 14-year-olds accompanied by their parents.

Afro-Caribbean party palaces... Though they lead rather different lives in Paris, the city's black African and Caribbean communities party together. The difference here is that most of the Caribbean people, called *Antillais*, come from Martinique and Guadeloupe, islands that are an integral part of France and offer classic French education, which has enabled *les Antillais* to become prosperous in the mother country. In contrast, most of the Africans are immigrants from former French colonies, and in spite of the tedious French boast that the country isn't racist, many of these people from Senegal, Mali, Cameroon, Zaire, the Ivory Coast, and Chad live in grim housing projects and earn very modest livings. It was this African immigration, which peaked during the seventies, that inadvertently made Paris the world capital of African music and gave birth to the city's lively Afro-Caribbean club scene. **Keur Samba** is the most venerable and dressy of these places, and the mixed but mostly black crowd dresses to the nines. This is the disco of choice for the African diplomatic community, so you need either to have a fat wallet or look like you have one to gain entrance and mix easily here. **La Chapelle des Lombards**, near the Bastille, plays what the club describes as tropical music, but at least half of it is Afro-Caribbean, and the same is true of the crowd. This is a serious party place, and you should dress the part, which means no sneakers or jeans. The **Café de la Plage** is another wildly popular dance locale in this category, with the advantage that you can retreat to the upstairs bar if the noise, smoke, or heat get the best of you on the dance floor downstairs. The crowd here is a little younger and funkier than at some of the other clubs, and the music menu of a given evening will also include a bit of soul, funk, and salsa. If you're a 35-year-old computer programmer, it won't be slumming if you come here, but you might feel a bit out of place. **Le Tango**, near the Bourse (Paris stock exchange), is a very sexy club; this is the place if you really want to dance hard. The music's fantastic, including reggae, soul, salsa, tango, you name it, and the crowd's very hot to trot. The suburb of Montreuil, on the eastern edge of Paris, is home to the city's two main Afro-Caribbean clubs, **Le Nelson** and **Le Cinquième Dimension**. Le Nelson is more African, while Le Cinquième Dimension draws an *Antillais* crowd and is a bit more upscale; both of them offer a sweaty, funky good time, and all comers are welcome.

Latino lightning... From Latin house to salsa, rhumba, merengue, and the tango, hip Paris is moving to a Latin beat, which is curious in view of the fact that France has no direct historical or colonial connection with any of these countries. Latin tunes, however, are the music of choice for the large number of young party people who detest techno and find house music a bore. One thing the Latino places have in common is that they're a reliable good time—people really come out to play, not to pose. The liveliest Latino club is **La Java**, a fabulously funky, old dance hall—Edith Piaf and Maurice Chevalier both sang here—in the ethnic cauldron that is the Belleville quarter of Paris. A diverse high-energy crowd comes here to really move it to Brazilian and Latin tunes. **Les Etoiles**, in the drab neighborhood near the Gare de l'Est, is the most popular salsa venue in town and attracts a cross-section of the city's Latin-American population. Latin fans should also check out what's on at **La Chapelle des Lombards** and **Le Balajo**; both often have Latino nights.

In search of Madame Butterfly... **Sinostar**, a sprawling Chinese restaurant just over the city line in the suburb of Le Kremlin-Bicètre, is an antic, exotic night out. It's usually about two-thirds Asian, but everyone is welcome, and the food, especially the dim sum, is quite good. During dinner you'll be serenaded by an Asian pop trio that specializes in seventies disco classics along with various Asian hits. You'll also have the pleasure of watching one of the most curious crowds of dancers in Western Europe; think middle-aged Cambodian beauticians getting down with Vietnamese teenagers and Laotian cabdrivers to the karaoke version of Diana Ross's "If There's A Cure For This." This is definitely a place to come with a group, which is what the Asians do and how they manage to drain bottle after bottle of Cognac, their libation of preference.

Taking it easy... If you're looking for a party environment that's not fashion-aggressive or excessively seasoned with attitude, there are plenty of places to go in Paris where you'll find good music, mixed-age crowds, and a lively night out. **La Cithea** is a popular, easygoing club near the place de la République that offers more attractive surroundings than are found elsewhere, including flattering, indirect lighting and good ventilation. A hip but friendly crowd turns up to listen to concerts—usually acid jazz—on Thursdays, Fridays, and Saturdays, and to dance to house music afterwards. **Le Neo** offers a similarly casual good time in its subterranean warren of cellars near Les

Halles; the music here varies, so you should call ahead if you're yearning for a quiet time, or want to avoid their rap, hip-hop, or funk evenings. **Le Casbah**, once an oh-so-cool place near the Bastille, has been improved by a fit of hubris brought on by a formerly too-nasty door policy; now they're generally welcoming. This place, decorated to resemble a North African *souk* is, as its name suggests, a pleasant spot to drink, hang out, and listen to tunes that follow the general, trendy, musical cocktail of Paris these days—to wit, a bit of soul, a bit of funk, a bit of acid jazz.

Life is a cabaret... Many people are confused about what to expect at a Paris cabaret, for the word can imply varied entertainment. Disabuse yourself of the idea that you'll cross paths with Liza Minnelli or Michael York; contemporary Paris cabarets offer generally wholesome, light entertainment that has nothing to do with the Berlin version popularized by the film. Most cabarets that survive in Paris today offer a classic mix of magicians; comedians; singers doing Piaf, Chevalier, and Brel; and mimes. At their best, these places, such as the famous **Lapin Agile** in Montmartre and **L'Ane Rouge**, offer an interesting night out and a very typically Parisian experience. Note, however, that Parisians frequent these clubs only very occasionally; the crowd will likely be heavy with visiting firefighters from the provinces, business people entertaining out-of-towners, and tourists. **Le Canotier du Pied de la Butte** is a wonderful place, especially for Piaf and Brel fans, and it's one of the rare cabarets frequented by the locals, including off-hour artists from surrounding clubs. **Le Caveau de la Bolée**, a minuscule bar in the Latin Quarter, draws a student-age crowd to its sing-alongs, and is a fun place to go on the spur of the moment.

Where to boogie with Brooke Astor... If you have a *Gigi* fantasy, there are still a lot of smarmy playboys in the Paris woodwork, and some of these places are not only fun but interesting for what they reveal about the French class system. **L'Arc**, with a glam setting overlooking the Arc de Triomphe, attracts a lot of yuppies from the very wealthy 16th arrondisement, as well as the tony suburbs of Neuilly, Passy, St.-Cloud, and Versailles on the city's western flank. Imagine what disco night would be like at the Greenwich Women's Garden Club…. Well, it's not as bad as all that, but you get the idea. Lots of boys in blazers, lots of girls with the telltale velvet headband holding back their bob cuts, expensive drinks, secret confessions. **Niel's**, just down the street, is a bit more sophisticated, with a rather more worldly, slightly older, and more cosmopolitan crowd. This is one of the rare places that draws well-heeled, young married couples. Single, professional French women feel comfortable coming in pairs, perhaps because of the clubby atmosphere—dark wood paneling and cushy leather armchairs—creates an atmosphere of (easily punctured) respectability. Who'd be happy here? Maybe seniors from Smith and Wellesley (but not Mount Holyoke), Wall Street types, merchant bankers of both sexes, airline pilots, and anyone with a trust fund. All things considered, it's a pretty good time. Ms. Astor would probably be most comfortable at **Castel's Princess**, and showing up on her arm is probably about the only way you'll get in. Just behind Saint-Germain-des-Prés— you'll know you're in the right vicinity when you see BMWs, Jeep Cherokees, Land Rovers, and pricey Italian metal parked at the curb—this place lays claim to being the snootiest club in Paris. Come if you want a minibar-bottle-size taste of someplace jet-setty, or if you're a woman wanting to meet a well-heeled boy toy to enliven a vacation. Attractive, well-dressed women get in with almost no problem, while it's rare that an unknown single gent gets past the ropes. Couples fare moderately better, too, especially if they hit the right balance between being naively New World and then rather indifferent about the whole thing—the worst thing you could do is whine, or wheedle, or hang around the door. Inside, you'll spend a fortune and find yourself in a crowd where men outnumber women two to one. Lots of babes, lots of heavy-drinking older counts of varyingly authentic pedigrees, lots of mobile phones. In an odd way, this place is a hoot, but don't bother with the restaurant.

All-purpose glamour… **Les Bains** remains just about the best of the younger-crowd, fashionable discotheques in Paris, and there have even been recent signs that its ferociously exclusive door policy is relaxing a tiny bit. It occupies a remodeled turn-of-the-century public bath where Marcel Proust once frolicked, with its main dance floor in the basement and a pricey restaurant at street level. The food served is indifferently trendoid, with several pseudo-Asian dishes, pastas, and salads, but eating here is a sure way of getting in and is actually sort of a bargain—you pay a flat fee of 270 francs, which includes dinner and the entrance fee. If the exclusivity issue doesn't put you off too much, you'll probably have a good time. The crowd's dramatically attractive—this is where the models come to let their hair down. The music, mostly house and garage, with the occasional rock 'n' roll night, is generally good.

Disco on wheels... La Main Jaune is the only roller disco in Paris, and it draws a very mixed but rather young crowd of wheel-happy folks to show off their high-speed stuff in the central skating rink. The music runs to soul and rap, and compared to many other such venues, the sound quality is pretty good. If you come with people who don't skate, they can hang out at one of the other bars or dance floors. The postmodern look here is Philippe-Starck cool, but this place doesn't have a lot of attitude and, who knows, this might be where you find your own little freeway to love.

Mondo dance halls... If you're in the mood for a big, thumping club with a mixed, just-add-booze-and-stir party crowd, Paris has some great places to go. The *grandmère* of the scene is **Le Palace**, a former theater, which has dominated the Paris dance scene for several decades. The coolest club in town when Halston was the coolest designer in America, it went through a couple of rough years, and is now gaining altitude again. **Le Bataclan**, a twenties dance hall near the Bastille, is sporadically the site of to-die-for one-nighters that attract the wildest fauna in town, while **Folies Pigalle**, an old burlesque theater near the Place Pigalle, packs a cool crowd of mixed gay and straight trendies who are more interested in a good time than throwing attitude. **La Locomotive**, also in Montmartre, is a gigantic club next door to the Moulin Rouge. Even people who shop from the Talbot's catalog would probably have a good time here—the crowd's well-scrubbed, often suburban, and the music runs more to James Brown than Masters at Work. The party here comes in three different flavors, too: diverse, live music on the first floor, a second-floor lounge for ballophobes, and the basement, where you go to cut loose.

Strictly ballroom... All of those places you've seen in old French films—where big-band orchestras are flanked by potted palms and ladies in low-cut evening dresses glide across the floor in the arms of gel-slicked gents—have vanished. Paris has become a virtual desert for people who love ballroom and other dancing. If disco or ethnic music doesn't turn your crank, you can have a night out at one of the fashionable-all-over-again *guingettes* (moored barges) found on the Marne River just outside of Paris. Come here for a glimpse of the France that illustrated your 8th-grade French textbook: the France of berets, accordions, Camembert, and endless red wine. The heyday of the *guinguettes,* was the *fin-de-siècle*, and they were a popular subject for Impressionist painters. After WWII, the advent of cheap airfares and television vastly diminished their numbers, but the few that remain are fantastic places to taste a uniquely Paris tradition and dance the night away. The classic **Chez Gegene**, in Joinville-le-Pont just outside of Paris (but easily reached by taking the RER A line to the stop of the same name), is wonderfully blowsy and draws an earnest crowd of regulars, many of whom have danced with the same partners long enough to become semiprofessional. The music runs from tango to forties and fifties swing, and absolutely all comers are not only welcome but comfortable here. Flowered shirtdresses and high heels are the look the ladies favor for a turn on the lacquered dance floor. A night at **Le Martin-Pécheur** is a truly unique experience, especially for twenty- to fortysomethings who like to dance. This *guinguette* attracts a cool crowd, especially during the good weather. The fifties and sixties retro looks rule here—striped sailor shirts and Apache scarfs. The trip requires a train ride and then a pulley-boat ride to the island where the *guinguette* is moored, so this is recommended only for intrepid Francophile nightlife fiends.

Boys and boys... Hard-core North American club boys will probably have mixed reactions to **Le Queen**, the glamo-rama gay disco of Paris. The physical plant's pretty good; it's a sprawling duplex space with many bars, and the music, depending on the night, is O.K., too. What will be very different is the crowd, which offers a telling mirror of Paris gay life. Aside from the surly gym-boys who come here after the macho bars close in the Marais, Paris gays still like to camp it up to a degree rarely seen on the other side of the Atlantic since such frivolity became de facto non-PC in the late seventies. So you'll see a lot of happy, young fashion victims, lots of suburban types wearing too-strong cologne, a few daring *BCBG* professionals, and a good number of buzz-top, neo-clones wearing muscle T-shirts. It's not really that easy to meet people here, because the posing factor is 9 on a scale of 1 to 10, but come here to dance with a friend. As a space, **L'Insolite** is a miserable place, a desperately crowded basement that's packed to the rafters on the weekend, but the crowd's friendly and mixed in age and outlook. The music can get on your nerves, though, because it's usually very top-of-the-pops, and most evenings end with a sloppy assortment of old French ballads. If you're itching to live out your own little *La Cage aux Folles* fantasy, you might try the **Scorpion IV**, a joyously fey place where you can wear eyeliner and big jewelry with impunity. If the median age were a determining factor, the **Club 18** would be more aptly named the Club 36—this inadvertently seventies, retro, basement dance club (the place just never changed) is one of the rare places in Paris where well-established professional types feel comfortable letting down their chignons. Wear a striped Oxford shirt, jeans, and expensive loafers, and you'll fit in just fine. If you like seriously weird places, **Le London** might be calling. What makes this place strange is that it's like a gay club in some remote French city; to wit, it's very French. Here the club plays a lot of French music that has understandably never crossed borders. The patrons are also prone to party games like conga lines. A mixed crowd, which includes a fair number of older men, comes here to whoop it up, French-style, on the weekends; it's pretty quiet during the week. Finally, the Sunday Tea Dance at **Le Palace** (see "Mondo dance halls," above) is still going strong after nearly 20 years. Though there's a whiff of time warp about this place for people coming from more progressive cities, the crowd's lively and mixed, and the place is perfect for preening and posing.

Girls and girls... Since **L'Entr'acte** opened, local lesbians are thrilled to have a new place to brandish their lipstick, which is what most of the crowd here is packing. This is a real disco, with plenty of room to dance to well-mixed techno and house music, or just hang out. Visiting women often find their French sisters a little standoffish, perhaps only because your pretty, new face threatens the order of a very cliquish community.

After-hours clubs... For dyed-in-the-wool party pups, inveterate noctambulists, or anyone who just wants to really cut loose during a vacation, the night in Paris lasts as long as you do. **Le Privilège**, the after-hours club in the basement of Le Palace, boogies until 6am—note, it's women only on Friday and Saturday—and almost all of the other major clubs keep you moving until at least 5am. There's also a thriving after-hours bar scene, with places like **Charly's Bar** and **Pandora Station** (See The Bar Scene) picking up the slack from 6am onwards.

The Index

L'Ane Rouge. Though you can come just for the show, this place is really dinner with entertainment. It's a rather good buy if heavy audience participation doesn't scare you off. The show usually includes all the elements of a fifties TV variety show: a singer, a magician, a ventriloquist, and a comedian.... *Tel 45 62 52 42; 3, rue Laurier, 75017; Métro Ternes. Open daily. 200F cover for show, 350F cover for show and dinner.*

L'Arbuci Jazz Club. A good bet if you're greedily trying to stuff as many great Paris experiences as possible into an evening, without spending a fortune. Don't expect anything especially radical, just good, local, mainstream jazz in the attractive basement club.... *Tel 44 41 14 14; 25–27, rue de Buci, 75006; Métro Mabillon. No jazz on Mon.*

L'Arc. French preppies and neo-aristocrats get down at this swanky and expensive club near L'Etoile. Don't bother with the restaurant, but note that the place is at its best during the soul-funk nights on Thursdays. Oh, and that Campari-and-soda you wanted will cost you 110 francs.... *Tel 45 00 45 00; 12, rue de Presbourg, 75016; Métro Charles-de-Gaulle-Etoile. Open daily. 100F cover Fri, Sat nights.*

Au Duc des Lombards. A central location in Les Halles and the fact that this club is open until 4am make it good for anyone feeling a sudden, desperate itch to listen to some jazz. The Tuesday night jam sessions attract an enthusiastic crowd of regulars.... *Tel 42 33 22 88; 42, rue des Lombards, 75001; Métro Châtelet RER. 50–100F cover.*

Les Bains. The ultimate fashion disco, this place always has a buzz, and if you missed Studio 54, come here for a Gallic approximation of the same ineluctable atmosphere. Beyond the models, the crowd's very mixed in terms of nationality, age, outlook, and sexuality.... *Tel 48 87 01 80; 7, rue du Bourg-l'Abbé, 75003; Métro Etienne-Marcel. Open daily. 100F cover Mon–Thur, Sunday; 140F cover with one drink, or 270F for dinner and cover Fri, Sat.*

Le Balajo. Though things have quieted down a bit since this was one of the most popular nondisco clubs in the eighties, it's still a wonderfully atmospheric place to shake your booty. The liveliest nights are the Latino retro ones, when a spicy mix of salsa, merengue, cha-cha, tango, and rumba is offered. And don't be afraid that you'll look like something out of an old "I Love Lucy" show on the dance floor—people come here to have fun rather than preen.... *Tel 47 00 07 87; 9, rue de Lappe, 75011; Métro Bastille. Closed Sunday. 100F cover.*

Banana Café. Popular, primarily gay cafe-bar near Châtelet with half-naked, male go-go dancers. A very young crowd.... *Tel 42 33 35 31; 13, rue de le Ferronnerie, 75001; Métro Châtelet. Open daily.*

Le Bar. In the basement of the sleek, modern Hôtel Villa, this is one of the most authentic Left Bank jazz venues, with a comfortable bar where you're likely to come across such first-rate American talent as Shirley Horn or Clifford Jordan. A good setting for a nightcap after a glamorous dinner.... *Tel 43 26 60 00; 29, rue Jacob, 75006; Métro Saint-Germain-des-Prés. Closed Sun. 120F–150F cover.*

Le Bataclan. Often the scene of 24-karat one-nighters, when there's something happening here it draws the best party crowd in town. Sniffy door policy, but well worth persisting. Go either very early or very late.... *Tel 47 00 39 12; 50, bd. Voltaire, 75011; Métro Voltaire. Hours and cover charges vary according to the event.*

Bilboquet. Tired, touristy left bank club offering New Orleans–style jazz and dinner in a Belle Epoque setting.... *Tel 45 48 81 84; 13, rue Saint-Benoît, 75006; Métro Saint-Germain-des-Prés. Open daily.*

Bus Palladium. The capital's premier rock-and-roll club, where everyone gets down as the night grows long.... *Tel 53 21 07 33 and 53 21 02 31; 6, rue Fontaine, 75009; Métro Pigalle. Closed Sun. 100F cover.*

Café de la Plage. Take a break from the dance scene downstairs at the upstairs bar at this thumping club where African, Caribbean, and Latino music reign. This place has more a neighborhood feel than other African-Caribbean clubs, and is mobbed on the weekend.... *Tel 47 00 91 60; 59, rue de Charonne, 75011; Métro Ledru-Rollin. Closed Sun. 100F cover Fri, Sat.*

Le Canotier du Pied de la Butte. A strong dose of authenticity in a neighborhood where it's hard to come by is only part of the appeal of this charming old cabaret where the bedrock trio of traditional French cabaret singers—Piaf, Chevalier, and Brel—were once regulars. The quality of the singing here is high, with wonderfully tear-jerking accordion music.... *Tel 46 06 02 86; 62, Bd. Rochechouart, 75018; Métro Anvers. Open daily. 190F cover before midnight, 80F after.*

Le Casbah. Handsome décor straight out of Rick's Casablanca cafe. Bar upstairs, disco downstairs. Soul, funk, and house sounds Friday and Saturday nights.... *Tel 43 71 71 89; 20, rue de la Forge-Royale, 75011; Métro Ledru-Rollin. Bar open daily 9pm–5am; disco open Thur–Sat 11:30pm–5am. Cover charge 120F Fri–Sat; 80F Tue–Thur, Sun.*

Castel's Princess. This place is ostensibly a private club, but maybe your charm will make them bend. Quasi-jet-setty, depending on the night, and fertile ground if you're prospecting for a young count or countess from a provincial city like Bordeaux. Lots of Brits in this plum pudding, too.... *Tel 43 26 90 22; 15, rue Princess, 75006; Métro Mabillon. Closed Sun. Cover charge at the club's discretion.*

Le Caveau de la Bolée. Stashed away in a snug cellar in the Latin Quarter, this place offers a bawdy night out with Anglophone tourists and students struggling to do their best with French music sing-alongs.... *Tel 43 54 62 20; 25, rue de l'Hirondelle, 75006; Métro Saint-Michel. 230F cover with dinner, 100F show only.*

Le Caveau de la Huchette. As much fun if you're 19 and have never been to Paris as it is if you're 45 and on your 10th visit. The ancient, vaulted cellar downstairs—there's also a pleasant bar on the main floor—is a great place to hatch a romantic reverie surrounded by French students with ingeniously tied scarves. The music is generally good, including players like Butch Reynolds, who once worked with Count Basie.... *Tel 43 26 65 05; 5, rue de la Huchette, 75005; Métro Saint-Michel. 60F cover Fri, Sat.*

La Chapelle des Lombards. Tropical ambience, music, and crowd at this brilliant club near the Bastille. The intriguingly mixed crowd includes party people from São Paulo to St. Louis, Düsseldorf to Dakar.... *Tel 43 57 24 24; 19, rue de Lappe, 75011; Métro Bastille. Closed Sun, Mon. 100F cover Tue–Thur, 120F Fri, Sat.*

Chez Gegene. Some soft starlit night, make an expedition to this nostalgic pleasure barge on the edge of town. The bar also serves simple bistro food, and the regulars eat steamed mussels with *pommes frites* and Beaujolais.... *Tel 48 83 29 34; 162, quai de Polangis, Joinville-le-Pont; RER Line A, Joinville-le-Pont station. Closed Mon. 50F cover.*

Chez Michou. Transvestite cabarets aren't to everyone's taste, but this one really is a riot, and the show's much funnier and more sophisticated than those in the more deadpan places with real ladies. A surefire gig that never fails to bring the house down is when the "girls" zero in on some of the dumpier patrons and feign finding them irresistible.... *Tel 46 06 16 04; 80, rue des Martyrs, 75018; Métro Pigalle. 550F cover, including dinner.*

Le Cinquième Dimension. An *Antillais* (French West Indian) dance palace, this club offers not only a good time but an interesting take on one of the most vibrant ethnic communities in Paris. A lot of French West Indians speak some English.... *Tel 42 87 38 63; Centre Commercial de la Mairie de Montreuil, 93100 Montreuil; Métro Mairie de Montreuil. Open Fri, Sun only. 100F cover.*

La Cithea. One of the rare Paris clubs without a cover charge, this comfortable space draws a friendly, mixed crowd to groove to live concerts, followed by dancing to mostly house

PARIS ⟍ THE CLUB SCENE

music. Drinks are cheap, too.... *Tel 40 21 70 95; 114, rue Oberkampf, 75011; Métro Parmentier. Closed Sun.*

Club 18. It's impossible to explain the vaguely bourgeois tone of this Donna Summer-ish vintage disco on the northern edge of the Palais Royal. You'll just have to drape a cashmere sweater over your shoulders and see for yourself.... *Tel 42 97 52 13; 18, rue de Beaujolais, 75001; Métro Palais Royal. Open Wed–Sun. 65F cover Fri, Sat.*

L'Entr'acte. Currently the busiest lesbian dance club in Paris, and because only about five women-only clubs exist in the city, the patrons would appreciate it if you didn't bring along a male pal, even if he's gay. Busiest on weekends, but lots of Parisiennes go out on Thursdays, too, to avoid the weekend crowds.... *Tel 40 26 01 93; 25, bd. Poisonniére, 75002; Métro Rue Montmartre. Closed Mon. 50F cover Sat after 1am.*

Les Etoiles. A no-holds-barred party palace that might have been airlifted from Santo Domingo, were it not for the fact that the shabbiness of this old dance hall is quintessentially Parisian. Live salsa music and a cover charge that includes dinner, which is usually rice and beans with pork stew or shredded beef.... *Tel 47 70 60 56; 61, rue du Château d'Eau, 75010; Métro Château-d'Eau. Open Thur–Sat. 100F cover.*

Folies Pigalle. The slightly tacky, slightly tawdry decor brings out the best in the hard-core gay and straight party crowd that roosts here. Good music and good cruising, because you can stalk your prey from a mezzanine balcony. The 40F drinks are relatively moderately priced.... *Tel 48 78 25 56; 11, Place Pigalle, 75009; Métro Pigalle. Open Thur–Sat. 100F cover.*

Le Gibus. Since the death of Jean Genet, the French haven't really understood skanky as a concept, but this old club on the edge of the proleteriat Place de la République has the slightly divey feel you'd expect from a heavy-metal place. The program varies nightly between house and techno and ear-slamming stuff.... *Tel 47 00 78 88; 18, rue du Faubourg-du-Temple, 75010; Métro République. Closed Sun, Mon. 30F–80F cover.*

Hot Brass. Though neither the location near the Parc de la Villette nor the space itself is optimum, this club draws a very hip crowd and has pioneered a place as the most progressive jazz venue in the city. If you're lucky, you can catch performers like Kenny Garrett and Roy Hargrove. Doors open at 8pm, and concerts start at 9:30pm. Come early for a good seat.... *Tel 42 00 14 12; Parc de la Villette, 211, av. Jean-Jaures, 75019; Métro Porte de Pantin. 100F cover.*

L'Insolite. A reasonably friendly and cruisy disco (whose name means "the bizarre") sets off an interior courtyard for people who prefer smaller clubs to big boom-boom rooms. A mixed-age crowd of regulars, ranging from bank presidents to bathhouse attendants, comes here to party and hunt new faces. Very crowded, very noisy, and very smoky.... *Tel 42 61 99 22; 33, rue des Petits Champs, 75001; Métro Bourse. 50F cover Fri, Sat.*

La Java. The contrast between the vague wistfulness of this classic Paris dance hall and the fact that it's now a high-powered and very popular Latino party venue is fascinating. A great place to meet people and dance off the *cassoulet* you had for dinner.... *Tel 42 02 20 52; 105, rue Faubourg-du-Temple, 75010; Métro Belleville. Closed Mon, Tues. 50F–100F cover.*

Keur Samba. Make sure your sleeve doesn't hide your Rolex at this pricey club with a door policy based on how expensive you look. Regulars wear tight dresses and expensive suits with the Armani labels left in place on the sleeve.... *Tel 43 59 03 10; 79, rue la Boetie, 75008; Métro Franklin-D.-Roosevelt. Open daily. 120F cover.*

Le Lapin Agile. Once a great center of bohemian life in Montmartre, which explains the framed sketches and caricatures of illustrious past patrons on the walls. You're best off here if you speak moderately good French. The atmosphere and the singing are enjoyable one way or another, but the poetry readings and comic sketches might leave you in the dark.... *Tel 46 06 85 75; 22, rue des Saules, 75018; Métro Lamarck-Caulaincourt. Closed Mon. 100F cover, 80F for students with ID cards.*

Le Lido. C'est Magnifique, the show at this dressy cabaret, is a favorite of Third World dictators, Japanese businessmen,

PARIS ◡ THE CLUB SCENE

and French plumbing contractors. In addition to the curvaceous charms of the Bluebell Girls, the show includes a bit of ice-skating and over-the-top special effects, such as an onstage waterfall.... *Tel 40 67 56 10; 166 bis, av. des Champs-Elysées, 75008; Métro George-V. 800F cover for dinner and show. 540F for show and champagne.*

Lionel Hampton Jazz Club. Though located in an ugly part of Paris—the area around the Porte Maillot was unattractively redeveloped in the seventies—this club tucked away in a Meridien hotel makes up for its lack of funk by being comfortable, spacious, and outfitted with state-of-the-art sound equipment. With the exception of nights when gospel, soul, or R&B are featured, the crowd tends to be older and often tie-wearing.... *Tel 40 68 34 34; Hôtel Le Meridien, 81, bd. Gouvion-St.-Cyr, 75017; Métro Porte-Maillot. 130F cover, including one drink.*

La Locomotive. Choo-choo your way to a big night on the town at this big club that's good-natured in a college-town kind of way. A good choice if you're going out with a group of people who all have a different idea of a good time—you can play the lounge lizard, be a dancing queen, or get down to live music, all in the same venue.... *Tel 42 57 37 37; 90, bd. de Clichy, 75018; Métro Blanche. Open daily. 65F cover.*

Le London. A basement disco in Les Halles that attracts a motley mix of mostly older French gay men. Gay discos in Paris in the sixties must have been like this.... *Tel 42 33 41 45; 33, rue des Lombards, 75001; Métro Châtelet. 50F cover Fri, Sat.*

La Main Jaune. Friday and Saturday are the big nights out for Paris roller-disco fans at this large, new club on the outskirts of the city. Even if you're a portly 35-year-old, you won't feel out of place here as long as you skate well.... *Tel 47 63 26 47; place de la Porte Champerret, 75017; Métro Porte de Champerret. Open Fri, Sat, and the nights before public holidays. 70F cover, 15F skate rental.*

Le Martin-Pécheur. A hip, jumping *guinguette* (dance barge) that attracts a groovy, young crowd that gets off dressing like extras from fifties French films. Usually you can count on a live band. Though getting here is a bit of a pain, it's well worth the effort; there's nothing like this at home.... *Tel 49 83 03 02; 41, quai Victor Hugo, Champigny-sur-Marne; RER line A, Champigny-sur-Marne station. Closed Mon. 40F cover.*

Le Moulin Rouge. There's still a trace of sincerity left in the show at this venerable Montmartre cabaret, and the club pleases its audience with a variety of rather Disneyesque cancan numbers. A lot of toothless fun and a place that even Tipper Gore might approve of.... *Tel 46 06 00 19; 82, bd. de Clichy, 75018; Métro Blanche. Open daily. 720F cover for show and dinner, 495F for show and champagne.*

Le Nelson. This is one major African party palace and a really good time if you want a workout. The crowd is friendly, totally uninhibited, and here to dance. Everyone's welcome.... *Tel 42 87 31 85; Place Jean Jaures, Centre Commercial de Montreuil Terminal 93, Mairie de Montreuil, 93100 Montreuil; Métro Mairie de Montreuil. Open Thur–Sun. 100F cover.*

Le Neo. A very Parisian crowd of mixed but generally arty locals comes to this atmospheric club occupying a series of crypt-like cellars near Les Halles.... *Tel 42 33 39 33; 21, rue Montorgeuil, 75001; Métro Les Halles. Closed Mon, Tues. 50F–80F cover.*

New Morning. The granddaddy of Paris jazz clubs, this is one of the most famous venues in the world, drawing top talent from Europe and America. Chet Baker was the unofficial house musician for years, a role now assumed by Archie Shepp. It's strongly advised that you book in advance, and note that the club accepts no credit cards.... *Tel 45 23 51 41; tickets: 42 31 31 31; 7/9, rue des Petites Ecuries, 75010; Métro Château-d'Eau. Hours depend on concert schedule. 110F cover.*

Niel's. There's a door policy here, but if you come during the week—generally a great way to get into such formidable places—you won't have any problem if you're dressed chicly. Media and fashion types like this place, which has a neo-Victorian look very likely inspired by Nell's in New York.... *Tel 47 66 45 00; 27, av. des Ternes, 75017; Métro Etoile or Ternes. 100F cover.*

Le Palace. This place is coming back smartly since Simply Red's Mick Hucknall and a bunch of other party pros took over from former owner Régine. A revised invitation list is bringing the key fashion crowd back, and the men-only Sunday afternoon Tea Dance remains a classic fixture of gay Paris. Check out *Barrio Latino* night on Tues.... *Tel 47 70 75 02; 8, rue du Faubourg Montmartre, 75009; Métro Rue Montmartre. Closed Mon. 50F–100F cover.*

Le Petit Journal Montparnasse. Though this club's a bit charmless, it's worth a visit if you're staying in the neighborhood and don't want to wander. The only way to score one of the front tables is to eat here; you're better off dining elsewhere and popping in for a drink. An older, elegant crowd sips snifters of cognac while listening to fine, contemporary, French jazz.... *Tel 43 21 56 70; 13, rue du Commandant-Mouchotte, 75014; Métro Montparnasse-Bienvenüe. Closed Sun. 100F cover and obligatory first drink.*

Le Petit Journal Saint-Michel. The split-level design of this club is uncomfortable and irritatingly limits sight lines, but the club attracts a young, professional crowd to listen to Dixieland music.... *Tel 43 26 28 59; 71, bd. Saint-Michel, 75005; Métro Saint-Michel-N.-D. RER. Closed Sun. 100F cover, including one drink.*

Le Petit Opportun. First-rate tunes and a friendly crowd packed into a series of medieval cellars make this one of the most popular jazz bars in Paris. The sidewalk-level bar is a popular hangout for musicians off-hours.... *Tel 42 36 01 36; 15, rue des Lavandières-Sainte-Opportune, 75001; Métro Châtelet. Closed Sun, Mon. 100F cover, including one drink.*

Le Privilège. Wild disco underneath Le Palace; popular with gays, lesbians, and straights. The club becomes the after-hours Kit-Kat after 6am Saturdays and Sundays.... *Tel 47 70 75 02; 3, cité Bergère, 75009; Métro Rue Montmartre. Closed Monday. Cover charge 100F.*

Le Queen. The name says it all about this the most popular gay club in Paris and also the most unjustifiably notorious club in Paris. There's a slightly capricious door policy; women are rarely admitted unless accompanied by at least two men.

Beyond Seventies Disco Mondays, there are many theme nights here, so ring up to see what's on.... *Tel 42 89 31 32; 102, av. Champs-Elysées, 75008; Métro George-V. Open daily. 50F cover Mon, 80F Fri, Sat.*

Le Rex Club. If you like techno, this is the place to come for some of the best deejays on the European club circuit. In addition to local star Laurent Garnier, the club frequently hosts visiting British club masters. You may observe that everyone here seems to be on something.... *Tel 42 36 83 98; 5, bd. Poissoniére, 75002; Métro Bonne-Nouvelle. Closed Sun, Mon. 50F–100F cover.*

Le Saint. The ultimate student's disco, with a lot of people who dance badly but have a really good time. The music includes something for everyone, ranging from Serge Gainsbourg to Latin house. Thursdays are good to avoid the weekend crush.... *Tel 43 25 50 04; 7, rue Saint-Severin, 75005. Métro Saint-Michel. Closed Mon. 60F–90F cover.*

La Scala. A play space for people who've just succeeded puberty but might still have trouble getting a credit card on their own. The music tends toward English pop groups, seasoned with a bit of retro disco and soul.... *Tel 42 60 45 64; 188, rue de Rivoli, 75001; Métro Palais-Royal. Open daily. 80F cover Mon–Fri, Sun; 90F Sat.*

Scorpion IV. Most of the clientele here would squeal in terror if they ever saw one of the arachnids this place has mysteriously been named after. A younger, often suburban crowd who likes to get all dolled up provides campy fun, nonetheless.... *Tel 40 26 01 60; 25, bd. Poissoniére, 75002; Métro Rue Montmartre. Open daily. 70F cover Fri, Sat.*

Sinostar. Two primary yearnings—for Chinese food and disco dancing—are satisfied in one place at this 650-seat restaurant in an adjacent Paris suburb. A fascinatingly mixed crowd of Asians, French yuppies, and banqueting friends get down over excellent egg rolls, dumplings, and seafood dishes. A perfect destination if you're curious about Paris's thriving Asian community and wonder what the top-of-the-charts in Taipei might be like these days.... *Tel 49 60 88 88; 29, av. Fontainbleau, 75013; Métro Porte d'Italie. Open daily. 160F cover, including dinner.*

Le Slow Club. In one of the city's best illuminated signs, neon dancers jut into the darkness over the rue de Rivoli, announcing this jazz club that almost everyone likes. The prevailing clientele is young, hip, and well dressed, and the place is often crowded on weekends.... *Tel 42 33 84 30; 130, rue de Rivoli, 75001; Métro Les Halles. Closed Sun, Mon. 60F cover.*

Le Sunset. A great spot if you're a serious jazz buff, this club features breaking French talent along with players who are building their reputations—the French act Julian Lourou, for example. Be prepared, though, for a quintessentially Parisian, smoky cellar, where it's often a good idea to arrive early.... *Tel 40 26 21 25; 60, rue des Lombards, 75001; Métro Châtelet. 50F–80F cover.*

Le Tango. This easygoing club is a great place to dance the night away. The crowd is cool; lots of young French fashion designers like to swan by. Fabulous music includes everything from salsa to top-the-charts pick hits from Kinshasa. Drop by on Sunday afternoons from 2–8pm for the weekly tango party.... *Tel 42 72 17 78; 13, rue au Maire, 75003; Métro Arts-et-Métiers. Open Thur–Sat. 60F cover.*

Montmartre Clubs

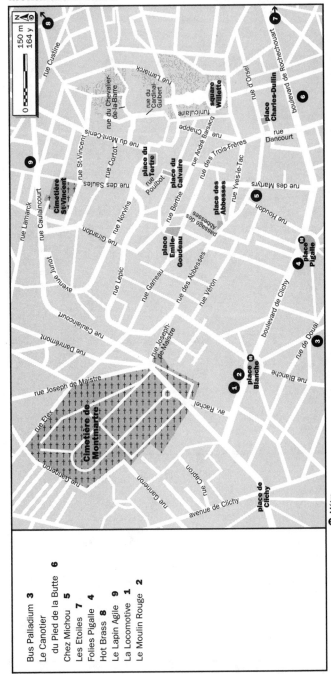

Bus Palladium **3**

Le Canotier
du Pied de la Butte **6**

Chez Michou **5**

Les Etoiles **7**

Folies Pigalle **4**

Hot Brass **8**

Le Lapin Agile **9**

La Locomotive **1**

Le Moulin Rouge **2**

Central Paris Clubs

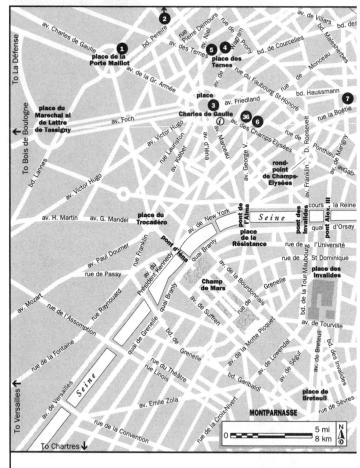

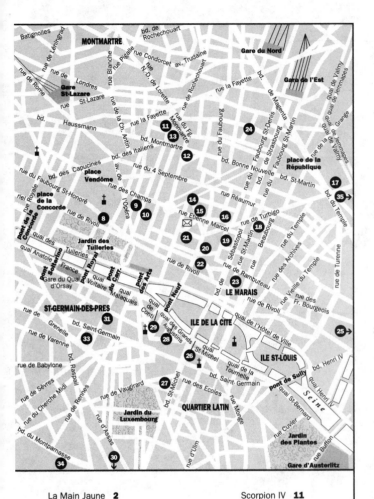

the bar

scene 2

The French are still much
shyer around hard liquor
than other Europeans.
They prefer the public
liveliness of cafes to the
quieter calm of a classic
bar. Still, Paris has a fine

array of smart nooks and crannies in which to nurse a single-malt Scotch—currently the *très chic* after-dinner drink—or belt back a bourbon.

Cocktail culture first flowered in Paris with the construction of the city's grand hotels in the 1880s. Because London was the first European beachhead for American bar culture, serving mixed drinks was considered an Anglo activity; Parisians preferred their wine and brandies. In *Les Années Folles,* what the French called the Roaring Twenties, the city crawled with American artists, scholars, and tourists. And it was then that Yankee-style cocktails became fashionable.

The Beaten Path

The last few years have seen something of a bar boom in the capital; the area around **La Bastille** has become the coolest drinking zone in town, with bars like What's Up Bar and the Bar des Ferailleurs. These two establishments are prime examples of the new Paris hybrid bar-club, where people sit at tables all night sipping drinks and listening to a deejay spin club-style house, rap, salsa, Afro-pop, and Algerian *rai* tunes. The **Marais** has become a notably high-spirited neighborhood for drinkers, and the area in town with the highest concentration of gay bars. **Pigalle**, traditionally a steamy pulse point in the Paris night, and the **Latin Quarter**, with its swarms of students and backpacking tourists, are the other areas of the city most hospitable to a bibulous night on the town. Lili La Tigresse, with its bar-top strippers and bordello-esque atmosphere, and the way-cool Club Club are the hot spots in Pigalle these days. If you want something more sedate, La Poste occupies a stunning turn-of-the-century town house and draws a mixed bag of French media types and starlets (including Lenny Kravitz's paramour *du jour,* Vanessa Paradis). In general, Pigalle's a bit funkier and less poseur-filled than the Bastille, and the Latin Quarter is even lower on the scale of formality and trendiness. If you venture for a tipple here, avoid the rip-off cafes around the Place Saint-Michel or along the souvlaki-stand-infested pedestrian streets running off it. Head instead for one of its many thriving pubs. The Café Oz, an Australian bar near **the Pantheon**, stocks a vast selection of brews from Down Under. And La Piano Vache, a classic student's bar near the **Maubert-Mutualité Métro**, draws a young crowd but is amenable to all comers.

What To Order

Curiously, in a country so renowned for its wines, beer is the libation of choice at most bars. The French know that they must never order wine anywhere except a wine bar or a pricey hotel because the quality is likely to be grim. And for many, cocktails are prohibitively expensive. A vodka and tonic or rum and Coke is likely to set you back an average of $10. The only cocktail that younger Parisians consume with any relish is the margarita, a tequila drink that retains a certain novelty value here, though no one is likely to break into a chorus of "Margaritaville" in a Marais bar. Cocktail culture, as such, is not as elaborate as in North America, so don't expect every bartender to know how to mix a Long Island Iced Tea or to keep in stock the latest black-currant-flavored vodka. To vary your normal tipple or go local, you could always order a Pernod or a Ricard—anise-flavored French spirits especially pleasant on a warm night. Krönenbourg is the most common French draft beer; it's a lager that's nearly as innocuous here as Budweiser is in the States. Pelforth, which makes good dark or amber beers, is also widely available. Perhaps the best common French-made draft in Paris is Meteor, which comes from Alsace, on the German border. Foreign beers, such as Heineken, Carlsberg, the Belgian Abbey de Leffe, and Kriek (cherry-flavored and much better than it sounds) are also served in most places.

Etiquette

The legal drinking age in France is 18, but no one pays any attention to it whatsoever. The same goes for the law that bans public drinking. As long as your behavior is within the decorous limits of Parisian taste, you should not have to worry about a *gendarme* tapping you on the shoulder. Except for the swankiest establishments, few French bars accept credit cards or traveler's checks. Tipping is at your discretion because service is included in the bill, but it's customary to leave a franc or two when you have a beer standing at a bar. Larger amounts are expected for higher tabs when you've been seated at a table or if you've imbibed in posh surroundings. Bars almost never have covers unless there's live music.

If the French continue to demonstrate a bewildering enthusiasm for many of the worst aspects of contemporary North American lifestyles—you'll be amazed that the city can support so many mediocre Tex-Mex places, and perhaps surprised to see so many malls on the way in from the airport—they are finally embracing one of the century's best Anglo-Saxon inventions: the Happy Hour. Practically all popular bars now have them, and in view of how stiff their normal prices are, it's worth checking out the discount hours at any place you like well enough to return to a second time. Most drinking places in Paris close at 2am, and those few that stay open later raise their prices after this witching hour. A small number of places serve nonstop (See Late Night Dining), but make sure you still have enough money left for a cab ride home. The Métro closes around 12:45 and doesn't reopen until 6am.

The Lowdown

Putting on the Ritz... Many of Paris's swankiest bars are in its hotels. The Ritz, of course, is an appropriately palm-filled setting in which to spend 75 francs for a flute of champagne. **Bar Vendôme**, a plush bar just inside the Ritz's Place Vendôme entrance, is open to non-hotel guests. Even though you may sport big hair and sneakers, you'll enjoy it more if you dress the part, which is to say as smartly as you can. This is a very attractively lit room with a pretty view of the hotel's interior garden where drinks are served when the weather is warm. Try to snag one of the banquettes, and dawdle over a well-aged Calvados or a glass of Châteldon, a rare and refreshing mineral water from the Auvergne region. The piano players are usually good, but beware the sometimes noisome and rather incongruous gypsy violinists. Also at the Ritz, the tiny **Hemingway Bar**, named in honor of the proudly two-fisted boozing novelist, is tucked away in the very back of the hotel. This intimate little room is the fiefdom of Colin MacPherson, a Scot who's won bartending competitions all over Europe. It's hard to say what Papa would make of the place today, because it has the air of a British men's club. Still, many regulars swear genial bartender Colin mixes the best martini on the continent, and the bar has an excellent collection of single-malt Scotch.

Just off the Champs-Elysées in the Hôtel de Vigny, **Le Baretto** is one of the best new bars that has opened in Paris in recent years. Sporting a Milanese decor reminiscent of the thirties, the bar serves chilled Prosecco and other Italian wines by the glass. The night crowd is hand-holding couples as well as young media and fashion turks staying here or in one of the other expensive hotels in the neighborhood. For low-octane imbibers, the espresso is delicious, and you can also munch on a tasty prosciutto or mozzarella sandwich if you fancy a snack. The bar in the **Hôtel Normandy** has lead-glass windows and comfortable, appealingly worn, leather sofas and tufted arm-chairs. Not far from the offices of several big French dailies and magazines, this friendly place pulls in a mostly suit-wearing crowd of scribes and bankers. A cab stand just a block away makes this a convenient preprandial stop. Cocktails are well-poured and -mixed, even if the elderly cocktail waiters can be a bit daft. For some irritating reason, the bar refuses to serve red wine by the glass; so come here in high spirits for a bottle of the same or a glass of champagne. **Le Forum** has a wonderfully French *temps perdu* feel to it, with a surfeit of faux marble, fluttering cocktail napkins, saucers of green olives, and salted cocktail nibbles. The bar opened in 1930, and though it has seen fits and starts of modernization several times since, it remains a quintessential cocktail palace with a menu of more than 150 concoctions. Busiest after work, this place is also a popular rendezvous for affluent Parisian professionals before and after the theater, opera, or a concert. Since the very trendy and very attractively renovated vintage art deco hotel Montalembert opened three years ago, the **Montalembert Bar** has become a Left Bank institution. Occupying a private corner of an airy room off the main lobby, the bar has a modern decor by design star Christian Liagre, which includes a fireplace, Asian screens, discreet lighting, and seating groups of sofas or armchairs. All of the *gauche caviar* (wealthy Left Bank liberals) come here, including fashion designers, writers, editors, and film and stage stars. Similarly chic and discreet is **Le Belier**, the bar at L'Hôtel, the pricey Left Bank hotel most famous as the place where Oscar Wilde died. This hotel is very much on the map for visiting Hollywood I-just-want-to-be-alone types. Don't come here for a scene as such, but for the velvety mood, the privacy, and the possibility of basking in a little bit of refracted starlight. Popular with a slightly younger, fashion crowd, **Le Bar**, the bar in the Hôtel Villa, is a flashy Philippe Starck–style place that has a reputation as one of the best jazz venues on the Left Bank. The bar itself is a pleasantly sleek place to work out with a swizzle stick while surrounded by polyglot foreigners in Japanese designer clothing. The ink-stained expatriate wretches who once frequented **Harry's New York Bar**, one of the first and most famous bars in Paris, have now been supplanted by English-speaking baby bankers and administrative assistants. But Harry's still mixes a mean Bloody Mary, and legend says the tomato-juice cocktail was invented here. One way or another, all of the drinks are well-made, and this place has a lot of authentic Edward Murrow-ish atmosphere.

Too cool for words... The Bastille, as the neighborhoods nearest the Place de la Bastille in the fourth, 11th, and 12th arrondisements are collectively known, is the epicenter of Paris cool, and the ballast of the crowd is a group of young-minded, fashion-conscious, creative types. Think designers, advertising and television people, photographers, artists, models, and a sprinkling of unconventional professionals who groove on this scene. Come the weekend, this chic comet attracts a suburban tail, but only the luckiest of them get into the **What's Up Bar**, a quasi-private playground for musicians (like M.C. Solaar, king of French rap), fashion designers (like Jean-Paul Gaultier and John Galliano), and supermodels (like Werner, the face of Hugo Boss). Though nondescript in decor, the bar is white-hot with fashion and music people, and the draw is the superb music. The best house and techno music in Paris is spun by star deejay Laurent Garnier and a regular assortment of the best British club spinners. But the tunes are for listening only; you can't dance here. You also have to arrive early to find a place to sit—preferable to standing. And have a drink elsewhere beforehand because service is maddeningly slow. Definitely a place to sport your bodypiercings and dress as urban-wild as you dare. **Le Bar Sans Nom** is another major point on the compass of Bastille hipsters, but this place ranks a bit lower with the poseurs than other clubs in the nabe. Fashion cadets, arty types, slumming young professionals from other arrondissements, and the occasional Japanese tourist stake out one of the appealingly shabby, old armchairs that furnish the place. The musical mood runs to funk, salsa, and reggae, and the crowd's mostly a beer-drinking one, though the bartenders mix a mean Bloody Mary. The **Bar des Ferailleurs** is a very switched-on place for people with attitude who live to party. A young, fashion-conscious crowd packs the place, perching on high stools at the bar or seated at tables where they pose and eyeball each other while chain-smoking over their beers. **Sanz Sans** is hip but more democratic and less likely to throw you into a clothing crisis (just wear black, anything leather, and don't look as though you've tried too hard). Perhaps taking a cue from Nell's in New York, this very popular Bastille bar has a turn-of-the-century bordello decor, with big gilt mirrors, red velvet chairs, and ersatz Old Masters on the walls. A trendy but tame crowd bellies up to the U-shaped bar and packs the tables while acid jazz and funk lace the background. If you want something a little less animated, go upstairs, which is also kitsched out with auction-house furniture. High-tech cruising is offered by a closed-circuit camera that follows the action up front and projects it onto a screen in back. As is true with many hot spots, on the weekends this place is invaded by *banlieusards*, Paris's suburbanite version of New York's bridge-and-tunnel crowd, so come during the week unless you want to view that scene. **La Flèche d'Or** is one of the more original and offbeat bars in the city. Occupying what was once a station on Paris's now-abandoned circular railway, the sprawling space was originally opened by a group of artists as a place to display their paintings and sculptures. A small bar has been added, and a deejay spins everything from acid jazz to reggae in a play booth that's tucked behind a sculpture evoking an old train. Due to its remote location, this place only draws a real crowd on weekends, but it's well worth the effort of getting here for anyone interested in an authentically artistic scene. Creative types and the odd star also show at **Le Reservoir**, a super-cool cafe-bar-restaurant near the Bastille with a vaguely Tarantino feel. The food is okay but nothing special, and music runs to jazz, Latin and soul, but table-hopping is the name of the game here.

Cool but not cruel... If you don't want to dress to kill (maybe merely to maim) the **Pub 64 WE** in the Bastille area is a good option. Youngish locals come by just to hang out, play pool, groove to a mixed bag of tunes, and chat. It doesn't matter what you wear here in this small, unassuming place, and people are friendly. The bar has a stand-up counter and tables, and several of the bartenders speak English. **Stolly's** in the Marais sells pitchers of beer for 50 francs, which is a bargain by Paris standards. An amusing decor of papier-mâché sculptures and a lively mixed crowd makes a popular bar. It's an intimate hole-in-the-wall, where you'll likely have to stand, but people are friendly and often English-speaking, making this a good place to trade tips about the city. The half-price happy hour from 4:30–8pm pulls in thirsty throngs from all walks of life.

Bacchanalia... You're in Paris and you love wine. No problem, right? Well, sort of. At almost any hour of the day or night, you can get at a *grand cru* somewhere in Paris, but if your dream is to guzzle Côte Rotie and listen to Mary J. Blige at the same time, it just isn't going to happen. The problem is the rigidity of French drinking habits. For them, a kir (white wine of nearly poisonous quality mixed with black-currant liqueur) is the only legitimate way to consume wine outside the confines of a meal, and a well-bred French person never consumes wine after a meal. This means that members of the purple-tongue club will need a little strategy to stay on the grape all night long. The obvious answer is the city's wine bars, though many of them close early. If you want to make a nocturnal tour of the vineyards of France without leaving Paris, **Le Café de Passage** is the ultimate late-night wine bar. An annex of the Passage, a wine-oriented restaurant in the same neighborhood, this place stays open until 2am, and a hip, sleek crowd loves the shadowy, postmodern decor created by indirect lighting, dark walls, and wicker armchairs. The taped jazz is a good aural backdrop to an especially good offer of Burgundies and Loire Valley wines, and the cafe makes appetizing light meals like lentil salad, sausages, cheese plates, and delicious chocolate custard for dessert. The funky **Clown Bar** is another of a late-night oenophile's best bets, because the bar serves until 1am and attracts an interesting herd. Popular with models and fashion designers, this place was originally built as a sort of canteen for the nearby *Cirque d'Hiver,* or indoor circus, which explains the beautiful Belle Epoque circus-themed tiles and all of the vaguely kitsch circus memorabilia. There is also good, simple food, which makes this an ideal stop for supper if you're going clubbing in and around the Bastille. Also near the

PARIS ◡ THE BAR SCENE

Bastille, **Jacques Melac** is one of the most convivial places for wine buffs in Paris. With his luxuriant mustache, Melac is a wonderful character who loves to tease and flirt. He's very serious about his wines, though, and this is a great place to sample bottles you've never had before, maybe over a plate of cheese and bread. The bartenders pour until midnight. The fact that Trotsky once drank at **La Tartine**, and that designers like Thierry Mugler do today, says a lot about the evolution of the Marais neighborhood, but the tobacco-ambered walls and appealing scruffiness of the place remain unchanged. Their by-the-glass selection is good and fairly priced, and they do a wonderful variety of *tartines* (open-faced sandwiches). **Willi's** and **Juvenile's** are dressy, well-run wine bars near the Palais Royal that are owned by the same talented British team of respected wine experts, Tim Johnston and Mark Williamson. Because the food's good at both places, they're very popular at noon, and then again as an after- work rendezvous for stylish, young professional types. **Le Rubis**, off the rue Saint-Honoré not far from the Place Vendôme, draws a similar crowd, mostly singles, and these people really like to put it away. Come summer, the bar stands old wine barrels out on the sidewalks as tables and the animated crowd pours out into the street.

BCBG (Bon Chic, Bon Gens) watering holes...

Novelist Charles Bukowski would not recognize the crowd in **Barfly**, the establishment that his novel inspired. Long-legged beauties and lupine playboys (the French definition of *BCBG*s or beautiful people) mix it up with a French movie and theater crowd. You come here to preen as much as to eat and drink, and though some might find the whole show a tad pretentious, it's fun if viewed from the distance of being a foreigner. Note, though, that reservations are esssential, because of a capricious door policy favoring the handsome, beautiful, and famous. Saudi princes, star athletes, media tycoons, long-stemmed Nordic beauties, public-relations empresses, and a lot of wannabes have made **Doobie's**, off the Champs-Elysées, one of the most fashionable night spots in town. The decor in this self-consciously exclusive place invokes an aura of a private club, and it's meant to, with the subliminal message being that you're lucky to have gotten in. The *hauteur* of the doorman and staff notwithstanding, this is an entertaining place to people-watch over a Scotch. The hip-hop soundtrack prevents it from becoming hopelessly stiff. It's not easy to mingle here, though, because you're immediately led to a table once admitted, and no one stands at the bar. Unless you're planning on showing up on Jack Nicholson or Madonna's arm—they're habitués—you should dress to kill, which means understated casual chic, as in a cashmere blazer or a killer little black dress. But beware the expensive drinks. **La Poste** is an attractive basement bar in a stunning 19th-century mansion that now houses a restaurant. Once the home of composer Hector Berlioz, the bar is a good bet in Pigalle if you want something quieter and dressier than the motorcycle jacket mode that prevails in this part of town. Beyond Vanessa Paradis, the kittenish actress, you've probably never heard of the many heavyweight French stars who come here to play pool and be seen, but they include Etienne Daho, a French pop star, and Arthur, a TV personality with a cult following. The Victorian decor under a tented ceiling sets off little black dresses and blazers with jeans to great advantage. The restaurant upstairs is filled with the same fashionable faces, but don't bother—the food's mediocre and expensive.

Hip places for singles... Hip but nonthreatening, **The Lizard Lounge** in the Marais serves decent food from its open kitchen, and the mixed, arty, heavily single crowd tends to linger at the table afterwards to drink. The split-level design—there's a heavy-gauge steel balcony—allows a choice between a little quiet and being in the thick of things. The mood along the long bar is very much that of the Marais—liberal, worldly, and easygoing. The basement bar has a pool table, and there's often a deejay playing mostly house music, but sometimes the lounge shows movies and sponsors theme nights. A bit more crowded and funkier, **Le Comptoir** is one of the most entertaining bars around Les Halles. The mood's slightly more Barcelona than Paris, with a Spanish menu of light meals and snacks, and a cracked-tile decor. On Friday and Saturday, it stays open until 4am and a deejay spins a nice mix of African, Latin, and house. The crowd comfortably includes everyone from 20 to 50—what matters is that you look like a gallery owner, a landscape architect, or a stylist. Located in the heart of the Marais, **Chez Richard** is a laid-back and fashionable bar that draws a rather more mature and better-dressed crowd than neighboring watering holes. Come here if you're thirtysomething, love Euro attitude, and desire cocktails. Inside, the bar echoes Barcelona with cracked tile work, gallery-style lighting, and modern art. Stay upstairs if you think you might like to meet people, or head down to the basement with a pack of friends. This bar mixes a mean margarita, and there's a good choice of beers, including brews from several Belgian abbeys.

If you'd rather go to a bar than to a club...

Certain Paris bars are as glamorous or lively as any nightclub or disco in town, the difference being that they're often less expensive and more relaxed. The atmosphere is wonderfully louche and colonial at the **China Club**, just a few steps from the Bastille. The mood's right out of Marguerite Duras's *The Lover,* a smoldering tale of illicit amour set in then-French Indochina. Don't bother with the mediocre and expensive Chinese food. Take a place at the downstairs bar or the busier upstairs one and absorb the scene, which is about as high-voltage glamour as Paris produces. Young wolves in Hermès suits perch their motorcycle helmets on the bar and chat up an international array of gorgeous women. The cigar service at the upstairs bar is much appreciated by striving young tycoons. **Le 9** is a rollicking bar that accommodates all ages—the bar plays old French songs and top-of-the-pops—on the Ile St.-Louis in the middle of the city. Respecting the prevailing tastes of their habitués, this musical selection usually tilts toward chart busters and Latin tunes. Popular with French yuppies, who are far friendlier here than elsewhere in the 'hood. Late at night—they're open until 6am—the crowd gets younger as people come in after a club outing for a last drink. The **Merle Mocquer** is one of the better places in Paris to catch new French bands; a group of some kind plays every Sunday night. This harmlessly rough-and-tumble bar also offers an excuse to discover one of the most charming and little-known corners of the city—La Butte aux Cailles. This funky, vibrant community is more like a village where folks drop in regularly to hang out over cheap beers. For something decidedly friskier, **Le Satellit Café** is a happening spot in the 11th arrondisement, one of the few parts of central Paris where younger people can still afford to live. The draw here is the fantastic mixture of world music, which means everything from Egyptian pop music to Algerian *rai* to reggae to salsa. The bar also serves good wine by the bottle, a plus for vinophiles. The crowd sports a lot of Jean Seberg and Jean-Paul Belmondo look-alikes.

Nocturnal cafe society... To the chagrin of nightbirds, most cafes close well before 9pm, but the difference between a bar and a cafe is mostly a matter of atmosphere and intent. Cafes draw a less slaphappy crowd; bars attract drinkers. Cafes very rarely play music, while almost all bars have some kind of tune cooking in the background. Generally, most Parisians head to cafes for relaxation, and to bars for a more animated good time. There are, of course, exceptions to this rule. **Angel Café** is strategically located near the underground mall at Les Halles. Food and drink service runs until 2am, making this a popular pre-club rendezvous for a techno-loving, predominantly gay crowd. From Thursday through Saturday, deejays tease the crowd into dance mode. The slightly fey sky-blue and fawn-colored decor corresponds perfectly to the slightly fey clientele. **Café Marly** sports a dramatic Napoleon III decor, with Pompeiian red walls and black trim. Though the food's rather ordinary, it's one of the chicest late-night scenes in Paris, with a high eye-contact factor. Best of all, its location in the courtyard of the Louvre offers spectacular views of the illuminated I. M. Pei pyramid from its terrace at night. And it's perfect for a light meal after a stroll in the newly renovated Tuileries gardens. Every neighborhood needs a living room, and **Café L'Industrie** is it for the trend-o-rama Bastille. The decor is a mishmash of artful flea-market finds and one-of-a-kind *objets* and posters. The cafe serves drinks and light meals, and if the food is nothing special, odds are you'll still have a good time using your salad as prop. After the now extinct Café Costes in Les Halles first proposed a whole new look—sleek and modern—for Paris cafes, dramatic, bi-level **Café Beaubourg**, designed by Christian de Portzamparc, was one of the very first to take the cue. The postmodern decor—travertine floor, ivory concrete composite walls and pillars, and a mezzanine around the main atrium—speaks of modern France, or the France of Philippe Starck instead of Hector Guimard (the artist responsible for the art nouveau Métro entrances). A great spot to visit alone, order a salad or an omelet, and read the *International Herald Tribune,* write postcards, and observe the crafty comings and goings of the local fauna. Start or end an evening here; it's always lively. At **La Palette** a mix of antique and art dealers and students from the adjacent Ecole des Beaux-Arts animates one of the more popular and authentic Left Bank cafes. Inside are gorgeous art nouveau tiles, and outside, a very pleasant terrace on a street corner that isn't completely befouled by car exhaust. As a nighttime venue, this place is most popular during the warm weather when the outside terrace is open, but it's also a fine setting for a solo cup of coffee on a winter's night.

See-and-be-scene cafes... **Café de Flore**, the former haunt of Jean-Paul Sartre and Simone de Beauvoir in Saint-Germain-des-Prés, rates a glowing mention in every Paris guidebook, and yet it still attracts one of the chicest and most powerful crowds in the city for lunch. At night, it's still aglow with big names. The waiters are cordial and prompt, and the food is unfailingly good. Such quality comes at a price; this is one of the most expensive cafes in the whole city, and many residents think it's scandalous that they dare to charge 45 francs for a glass of ordinary Bordeaux. Local opinion holds that **Les Deux Magots**, neighbor to the Café de Flore and equally expensive, is slightly flashier, but they're quibbling. In a fashion equation, it's akin to the difference between Armani and Versace. Where the Magots holds the better cards is during the summer months, when its spacious terrace overlooks the beautifully lit church of Saint-Germain-des-Prés across the street. Nonsmokers are also catered to here in an enclosed sidewalk terrace where smoking is verboten. A favorite rendezvous of the hawkeyed international fashion crowd, this cafe's a great place to take your most daring club outfit for a test run. **Le Fouquet's** on the Champs-Elysées is an obviously chic and expensive place to linger over a cognac after dinner. Though Le Fouquet's used to be a watering hole of James Joyce, the crowd these days runs to media tycoons, rich Arabs, enthusiastically made-up ladies, and French show-biz types. This is the stop for an after-dinner coffee if you're strolling home down one of the most famous avenues in the world. Expect to pay a pretty penny for the pleasure of rubbing elbows or egos with the global rich.

Late-night cafes... **Pause Café** is where Bastille hipsters cruise in for a time-out cup of coffee and mineral water or to regroup between bars. This is an easygoing, ordinary cafe in the midst of the best after-dark neighborhood in Paris. Peer out at the passing parade across your formica-topped table through big picture windows. **Le Zephyr** is not so much a destination as a fine reference point if you're planning to hang near Le Palace. The neighborhood is unfortunately infested with most of the worst fast-food chains in the world, including a newly minted TGIF. But this cafe is a respite from the commercialization and ideal for lazing about over a coffee or a beer.

Cafes for conversation... At **Le Petit Fer à Cheval**, English-speaking bartender Xavier is an amiable wise-cracker who holds court with his regulars, an interesting, international clientele, from behind the cozy horseshoe-shaped bar. At this popular Marais cafe you can get light meals, including a good *plat du jour*. The whole place has a wonderful eternally Parisian feel to it. On your own, settle in at the bar over a draft beer and a conversation will surely follow. The clientele is interesting and international. Far from the madding tour buses that congest this part of town, **Le Sancerre** is a bustling neighborhood cafe that pulls an arty local crowd with nary a dowager from Düsseldorf in sight. The decor is marked by a mermaid overhead, and in good weather, the terrace out front is a great spot to spend an evening over a Pernod and a heart-to-heart talk. This is one of those rare places that's fashionable without trying too hard, and it's a great pause while exploring this part of the city after dark. **Le Select** was one of the bright lights on the scene when Montparnasse was Paris's artistic epicenter during the twenties and thirties. This cafe is the only spot that retains any of the area's original glamour. The interior is original with vintage thirties wrought-iron fixtures, raw wood tables, and a wonderful glass skylight. The crowd is diverse and artistic.

Margarita madness... For margarita aficionados, frozen, presweetened lime juice—fresh limes don't grow in France and imported citrus is expensive—is intolerable in that most famous tequila concoction. In Paris, margaritas are also sullied by rotgut, bar-brand tequila, stingy portions, and a lack of ice. If you're yearning for a salt-rimmed margarita, though, **La Perla** is the place. Ceiling fans, a long wooden bar, and picture windows make this Tex-Mex restaurant-bar a dinner or post-dinner stop. The service is friendly and mostly bilingual, and in addition to serving very good margaritas, the bars stocks a full range of Mexican and other foreign beers.

Jazz holes... These bars offer you a chance to get a good dose of jazz without committing yourself to a whole night in a jazz club. **Le Bar** in the Hôtel Villa is stylish, comfortable, and offers live music. The provocative orange and purple decor signals that you're a long way from the Louis-the-Something world of the grand hotel bars, but, its contemporary chic notwithstanding, Le Bar has happily aided and abetted the Saint-Germain jazz tradition. This is a great place to drop in for some first-rate jazz with your nightcap. **Le Birdland** in Saint-Germain-des-Prés is a wonderful only-in-Paris place, a snug little hideaway with red-velvet stools, a splendid collection of single-malt whiskies, and one of the largest libraries of jazz recordings in Europe. A mature, well-heeled crowd—the Saint-Germain night scene is expensive—frequents this place, but almost everyone feels comfortable here. If you'd rather nurse a single-malt Scotch and take in some tunes than hit a club, this is a fine option. The play list runs from classic to the funkiest modern sounds, and the staff is reasonably responsive to requests.

Latin rhythms... While salsa and Afro-Caribbean music become ever more popular in Paris clubs, **Jip's** is the best bar in the city where this music rules. With its Day-Glo murals, this is one of the funkier and livelier bars in Les Halles. It flies the flag for Afro-Cuban music in Paris and makes you more susceptible to its charms with a long list of generously poured rum-based cocktails. Somewhat sedate during the day, when good Caribbean dishes are served at noon, at night this place blasts off as one of the most popular bars of the city's African and West Indian population.

In need of a heavy-metal fix... If Tonya Harding is your idea of a babe, this is the bar for you. While heavy metal is nowhere near as popular in France as it is in Northern Europe, especially Germany, the **Ministry** is the center of the small but raucous Paris heavy-metal scene. Your parents probably wouldn't enjoy this bar very much, but it could be the only chance you'll have during a trip to Paris to hear some old Kiss favorites. Artfully applied cobwebs, a skeleton or two, and a couple of gargoyles create the mood, along with the young crowd of thrashers who might be Alice Cooper's children.

So much beer, so little time... As they do with most things in life, the French adopt a connoisseur's pose when it comes to beer, and it's in this search for quality brews that they tip their hats to their northern neighbor—Belgium. At **L'Académie de la Bière** this beer-hound's haven offers ten brews on tap and throws in another 150 by the bottle for good measure. Habitués insist that some of the best are the least known—including libations from Senegal, Gambia, and other far-flung corners of the world. The food's decent too; try the mussels served with french fries. The only conceivable reason you might naturally end up at **Bar Belge** in this somewhat remote neighborhood of the 17th arrondissement is if you decided to take a stroll here after scuffing through the flea market at the Porte de Clignancourt. Otherwise, the most venerable Belgian beer bar in Paris attracts a mostly young male cross-section of connoisseurs in training. The atmosphere, however, is very pleasant and not in the least bit frat house. If you do love your brew, choose from more than 50 Belgian selections. Because they serve until 3am, a wonderful mix of weirdos collects here in the wee hours, especially on weekends. Though the surrounding neighborhood goes rather quiet at night, **Au General Lafayette** is always busy with people from all over town who know its reputation for an outstanding menu of high-quality suds. The bar carries a vast range of beers, and their Belgian selection is particularly interesting. Come here to hang out after dinner; the atmosphere is relaxed and the setting is comfortable with *trompe l'oeil* paintings on the ceilings, good lighting, and plants. **Le Sous-Bock Tavern** serves more than 400 beers, including 12 on tap, and some 30 whiskeys, along with snacks recommended more as stomach sponges than good cooking. It's less appropriate for a *tête-à-tête* than a night out with a band of friends, but with its convenient location and late serving hours, this is a hassle-free address for just about anyone.

For an intellectual rendezvous... The great intellectual traditions attached to Paris cafes and bars have recently been on the wane. It is, after all, easier to watch Björn on MTV than it is to invent a new philosophy. Further, the political landscape in France today, where the Socialists are barely distinguishable from the Gaullists, doesn't inflame passions the way it once did. If you'd like to repair to a prime place to discuss politics or prenatal care, **L'Art Brut** is the place. Its distressed decor (the facade's been hammered together from old pieces of sheet metal and wood and the interior has exposed ventilation ducts and a bathtub screwed to the ceiling as a sort of unique lighting fixture) may first strike you as a bit bleak, but this is actually a rather convivial place. Because it's frequented by disheveled writers, artists, and professional brooders, it should come as no surprise that drinks are cheap.

Cyber-cafes... *Mais, oui,* Internet junkies needn't be deprived of cyberspace while in Paris. Come to one of the growing number of Internet cafes if you want to check your e-mail, communicate cheaply with pals at home, or share something in common with the person at the neighboring console. Most of the cyber-cafes aren't exactly places to yuck it up, but maybe you want to tell your mom about dinner last night, remind your best friend to change the kitty litter, or just have a pretext for hanging out. **Café Orbital**, now in two locations near the Bourse (Paris stock exchange) and across the street from the Luxembourg Gardens on the Left

Bank, was the city's original online cafe. It attracts a mixture of earnest business types and miscellaneous people who want to play and chat at the six machines in this place. While this isn't a cafe you'd really want to hang around in unless you came to surf, the new branch is a bit livelier. **Web Bar** in the Marais is busy and ideal if you want a bit of house or jazz bopping in the background, and maybe a mug of beer to inspire you as you find out if your e-mail buddy in Auckland has sent along a message. This being the Marais, there's art on the walls and a lot of people are wearing black. The hardware isn't fantastic, but if you're in a good mood and have nothing more pressing to do, this place is ideal. **Zowezo** near Pigalle is where to head when you've got an urgent message to send but you're feeling frisky and want to hit the party trail as soon as you've logged off. This is the place to send and pump up a mood at the same time. Groove to the salsa and reggae tunes, scarf some pasta, and swill a Caribbean cocktail at the zebra-striped bar.

Student dives... Even if you're not a student, many of their meeting spots are some of Paris's most convivial drinking locales. As their traditional Latin Quarter haunts have become more commercial and increasingly gentrified, many students now frequent bars and cafes in less expensive, outlying areas. On weekends, it seems all art, fashion, architecture, or graphic-arts students in Paris find their way to **Lou Pascalou**, an off-the-beaten-track bar. The decor might be described as nondescript if it weren't so authentic—cracked-tile floors, mirrors, tables on cast-iron bases. The big terrace out front is packed during fair weather. Fans of French films will recognize **Le Piano Vache**'s genus immediately: the classic student's bar. Come here to savor the smoke-stained walls, old wood beams, and the chatter of the bright-eyed and appropriately threadbare young crowd. The three rooms fill quickly in the late afternoon—the big corner tables are especially sought after—and remain full all night. The walls are plastered with old posters. A sign of the times is the MTV monitor, but otherwise this place has a charming pre-war feel. A frayed scarf and a copy of the ponderously serious French daily *Le Monde* are *de rigueur* accessories. Though **Polly Magoo's**

is a small, smoky, shabby place, it had a reputation as a bona fide pickup joint during the sixties and seventies. Today it's frequented more by earnest biology students than guys on the prowl. Parisians who were students in the sixties have a certain affection for this bar because it was often the scene of the preliminaries to many a passionate evening. Though the great selection of beers at **Pub Saint-Germain** includes a full array of Belgian Abbey brews, you can also get a decent steak with fries or a salad if you need a little ballast. Convenient and friendly, it's also a help that this bar accepts all credit cards, in case you need to save your last hundred francs for a cab home afterwards. While far from a Manhattan Upper East Side fern bar, **Le Violon Gingue** in the Latin Quarter has definite Mr. Goodbar overtones. On the face of things, it's an innocuous-looking, Yankee-style college bar with wood paneling and U.S. football playing on a screen in back. Every night becomes a frat party here, as backpackers, local students, and French boys on the prowl come in to slurp cheap beer and search for short-lived romance.

If your inner child is a hippie... Almost 30 years ago, the Latin Quarter percolated with social ferment, and head shops did a brisk business. Today, of course, many former rock-throwing students are worrying about their own children's enthusiasm for techno music and high-grade pot. Still, if you're desperate to find a place where you can wear your Earth Shoes without anyone snickering, **Le Bar Dix** near the Odéon is a snug and very popular Left Bank drinking den. Along with *Soixante-Huitards* (68-ers, as hippies are known in France), the crowd here is students of all ages from all over the world. On the street level, intense types discuss the fate of the sea turtles in the South China Sea at candlelit tables, while the cellar downstairs is a bit more riotous, as people throw back pitchers of the excellent sangria that's a house specialty.

Parlez-vous anglais?... Unless you speak French, one of the best ways to meet people is to frequent the bars and cafes favored by the capital's 100,000 native English speakers. They're an intriguing group, hailing from places as diverse as Durban, Denver, Alberta, and

Auckland. Some were posted to Paris by a faraway home office or a national diplomatic service, while others fell in love with the city, came here to paint or write, got home only to discover that it was more than a vacation romance, and came back for more. They're usually only too happy to tell you their stories and hear about what's happening back home. Though hundreds of dreadful American-style places continue to sprout around town, it's the Irish, British, and, recently, Australian pubs that offer the most atmosphere. Both branches of the Aussie **Oz Cafe** are young and lively. Both have an excellent list of Australian wines and imported beers like Melbourne Cascade. Ersatz Aborigine paintings hang on the walls, and a baby crocodile stands sentinel over this friendly, popular bar much frequented by Aussies, Kiwis, Brits, and Yanks. With the bare-bones charm of the local pub in a small Irish town, **Connolly's Corner** is perennially popular with English-speaking residents of the Latin Quarter, along with a number of funky French students and arty types. With Guinness and Murphy's on tap, the mood's always lively here. An amiably enforced local tradition prohibits customers from wearing neckties. If you chose to challenge it, yours will be confiscated and added to their dangling collection. Many Parisian connoisseurs of Guinness stop by **Flann O'Brien's**, an affable and well-located Irish pub. A lively crowd of regulars—this is the kind of place where someone might suddenly start singing an Irish ballad—come in to play pool, throw darts, tell tall tales, and listen to live Gaelic tunes. **The Frog and Rosbif** is a boisterous English pub whose name is a play on the slang for what the English call the French and vice versa. Located on a sleazy but bustling pedestrian street near Les Halles, it fills up nightly with an international mix of fans of its micro-brewed ales. Bearing silly sounding names—Inseine, Parislytic, and Dark de Triomphe—most of them are pretty good, as is their pub food, including ploughman's lunches and baked stuffed potatoes. The best turnout here is when there's live coverage of rugby and soccer matches.

For a wee bit of Ireland... **Kitty O'Shea's** is an attractive Irish pub and a favored hangout of French and foreign yuppies working in the heart of town. In addition to a full roster of Irish and foreign brews, there's excellent pub grub in the first-floor restaurant. The sausages and brown bread are imported from Ireland, and the bar also makes satisfying roasts and stews. With its central location and relaxed atmosphere, this is a good place to pop in for an after-dinner drink when you've been to a dressy restaurant but want to wind down for your nightcap—maybe a tumbler of Irish whisky. Live music plays nightly at **Molly Malone's**, from traditional Irish bands to local soul singers. This is a popular after-work spot for people employed in the surrounding advertising- and glamour-industry offices; the crowd grows rowdier and more casual later in the evening. Nonsmokers may find the ventilation wanting. **Quigley's Point** is an all-purpose Irish pub located rather incongruously at the head of one of the hottest fashion shopping streets in Paris. Pop in for a pint, and sit on a high stool at one of the saloon tables, or opt for more discreet surveillance from the booths along the wall.

A fine chance for romance... Le Rosebud is an impeccable little bar where the waiters wear black ties and take their work very seriously. They serve well-mixed if rather pricey cocktails, to be sipped against the jazz playing in the background and toyed with as you make eyes at the object of your affection. You catch a whiff of old bohemian Montparnasse here, as well as a stiffer gust of the new Montparnasse, which has recently become a business district. Envision a weird hybrid of New York's Greenwich Village and Upper East Side with everyone speaking French. At **Café de la Mairie**, the illuminated stone lions guard the torrents of the big fountain in the middle of the Place Saint-Sulpice at this very popular Saint-Germain cafe. On a warm summer night, the whole square becomes part of the cafe, and there are few better places to moon at Paris and people-watch. Inside, it's smoky and crowded, but the second-floor room is ideal for writing a letter to an old friend or gazing into the eyes of your amour.

In a Times Square state of mind... Trashy and flashy, you either love Pigalle or hate it. For real city lovers, to say nothing of people who're curious about Paris, the streets and boulevards running off the Place

Pigalle offer highly textured contrasts. This part of town is the traditional center of erotic entertainment, (peep shows, bump and grind) and a major middle-class European tourist neighborhood—hence the buses from everywhere from Finland to Portugal lining the avenues. It's also an artist's neighborhood and one of the trendiest party regions of Paris. **Lili La Tigresse**, a cheeky, modern strip bar, is a place where ladies won't feel uncomfortable. The whole place is meant to be sort of a send-up of the real thing, though, which makes it popular with an oddball crowd of young trendies, woozy businessmen who don't get the joke, and slightly bewildered tourists. If the frenzy downstairs gets to be too much for you, the upstairs bar is a little calmer. Busiest on weekends as a pre-club hangout, it's also fun during the week. Formerly a B-girl hangout, **Club Club** is now a two-level bar frequented by artists, writers, and other creative types who've been moving into this area. The first floor's preferable because the basement's rather claustrophobic, and the decor is haphazard, with low lighting and street-scavenged furniture. During the week, there's a different happening every night—maybe a poetry reading or a showcase of video clips—while a deejay spins Afro-jazz and Latin music on the weekends. Don some engineer's boots, jeans, a big, wool pullover, and a pea coat and you'll fit in just fine. **Le Moloko** is not quite as cool as it used to be, but this bar is still worth a stop if you're in the 'hood. Drinks are steeply priced, and a lot of the more authentic local trendies have moved on to greener (seedier) pastures, but Saturday night is striptease night, and the shaking booty draws a jolly crowd of French and foreign oglers. There's a minuscule dance floor downstairs, with music from the reasonably well-stocked jukebox.

The best biker bar in Paree... If you're missing the hog you left behind, come to **La Taverne Phify's** to commiserate with like-minded company. Phify's is about rock 'n' roll, Harleys, and slightly off-center *King of the Road* fantasies. Because a lot of 40-plus French movie stars and singers share these enthusiasms, this place also generates a bit of starlight. The reason you'll find it interesting is that the mix of Kerouac and Camus is thought-provoking, if not entirely natural, and because it's one of the rare bars in Paris where you'll feel completely natural wearing jeans.

On the wild side... Kurt Cobain would have loved **Le Pick-Clops**, which serves a sloppy good time to a hardcore party crowd in the Marais every night. Peek in the door if you're curious about the French equivalent of white trash, and step inside if you identify with the surly-looking, trendy types who like their fun low-rent. The walls are covered with mirrors and bright paint, table tops are genuine Formica, and the crowd of young trendies shouts at each other above the din of rock music. No place for the timid.

Kitschiest bar in town... If you're a fan of Pierre and Giles, the team of artists who've elevated kitsch to an art form in Paris and whose style may be familiar via Jean-Paul Gaultier advertising, you'll love **Le Leche-Vin**. Nothing indicates the visual mayhem within, but step inside and you'll be amused, fascinated, appalled, or maybe a combo of all three, by the funky weirdness of a place that is packed solid with every conceivable kind of popular religious icon from all over the world. Buddhist spirit houses jostle weeping virgins, and Santa Claus puts in an appearance as well. The whole effect is about as droll as the clientele, a hip mix of irony-appreciating gay and straight club people, students, and tourists. Note that the prevailing theme of chaotic, tongue-in-cheek piety gives way to hard-core porn in the toilets.

Where to go after last call... There are those times, especially when you're on vacation, when you just don't want the party to end. Paris offers a variety of places where you can get a hold of just one more after most of the clubs and bars have closed up shop. **Le Dépanneur** is an ersatz American-style diner that serves drinks, salads, sandwiches, and attitude round the clock. The super-cool young crowd—men in motorcycle jackets and women with legs to there—pose in the smoky din for hours on end. **Charly's Bar** is perhaps the best post-club, after-hours bar in Paris. All the house music fans of the capital seem to collect here to keep the beat moving. During the week, a student-heavy crowd takes in the "M*A*S*H" decor—camouflage netting, soldiers' helmets, and Asian artifacts. On the weekend the place really jumps. The twee name of **Pandora Station** tells nothing of the action here because this is one of the liveliest and most interesting bars in Paris. No one can explain the origins of the unfortunate movie-lot-jungle decorative scheme, but no one cares, either. This floating crowd of night people, including dancers from the Moulin Rouge and the Lido, pre-club hipsters, and neighborhood party people, likes a no-holds-barred good time. Regulars go for the potent house cocktails made with rum and fruit juice.

For lovers of legend and literature... Many Americans continue to associate Paris with the Lost Generation, and their affinity for writers like Ernest Hemingway and F. Scott Fitzgerald has become a useful marketing tool for some otherwise pretty banal bars and cafes. If you really want to brush up against some of this fading Roaring Twenties atmosphere, **La Closerie des Lilas** in Montparnasse is probably your best bet, but be warned that drinks are expensive and the staff is churlish. The cruelly maligned old sod that the place is named after would have appreciated that the **Oscar Wilde** bar, an Irish pub near Les Halles, serves until 4am. Calm enough during the week, when regulars sip from the pub's fine offer of Irish whiskeys, this place becomes something of a mating scene on the weekends. The ground-floor bar is calmer and more comfortable than the raucous downstairs counter. Sharing much in common with sister establishment Kitty O'Shea's, **The James Joyce** is an attractive if dressy place with a stock of Joycean memorabilia and classic Irish decor, much of it authentic and imported from Ireland. A popular spot for Sunday lunch, this place draws a shirt-and-tie crowd in the evenings.

Where the boys are... If you're coming from a switched-on city like Seattle, Toronto, or Miami, the gay scene in Paris may be a bit of a letdown. Though the French pride themselves on their tolerant attitude toward homosexuality, Paris is a resolutely bourgeois city; many gay professionals don't take part in the scene, preferring to socialize among themselves at private parties. Many of those who do go out still adhere to muscle-boy clone stereotypes, which are on the wane in many North American cities. The Marais is the heart of Paris gay life, and **Amnesia** is rather less heavy than other Marais watering holes. This place offers chairs and tables as well as barstools, and welcomes women. Windows opening onto the street and gentle lighting create a relaxed rather than furtive mood, and the place draws ponyskin car coats and Harris tweed jackets as well as leather bombers. **Le Central** is the oldest gay bar in Paris. It's also one of the most French, with charmingly awful French pop music and sad ballads mixed with the house music. Still, the crowd's friendly and the mood's relaxed. Breaking ranks with the dark, techno style of many Paris gay bars, **Cox's Café** is a new bar that follows the model currently in vogue in London's Soho. Big, half-frosted, glass windows; fresh flowers; a regularly changing decor; and even a chance to surf the Net on two computers. **Le Duplex** features art exhibitions in this small bar on the northern fringes of the Marais. Here it's mostly a younger, postmodern, gay crowd that can get a bit cliquish. At the three-level **Le Piano Zinc** bar in the Marais, it's a bit claustrophobic but a lot of campy fun, with a pianist and live singers performing in the basement and a happy crowd that likes to join in. Women are welcome, too. **Le Trap** is a late-night stop and a small, friendly place. This bar is all that remains of the once-thriving gay scene in Saint-Germain. Film clips and videos are screened at the ground-floor bar, while a circular staircase leads to a shadowy and more intimate mezzanine. There are gym boys in Paris, too, but a *La Cage aux Folles* set still thrives, and they're major patrons of **Banana Café**, a popular cafe-bar in Les Halles. Come the good weather, the terrace out front is packed with practiced poseurs, while in the evening there are go-go boys on the bar from Thursday through Saturday, and people attempt to dance between tables. Scorned by the macho brigade, this place is a four-year-old hit with hairdressers, drag queens, fashion tarts, and teases. It has also recently become chic with straight French preppies. **Le Quetzal** is the most popular serious cruise bar in Paris, but it's a rather charmless place. The core clientele is buzz-top, muscle-boy, Parisian clones, but lots of foreigners and French from the provinces lighten things up a bit. **Le Bar du Palmier**, once the most popular gay disco in

Paris during the seventies, is now one of the largest and busiest bars in town. It's a popular place, despite the fact that it has all the charm of a Chevrolet showroom on Christopher Street. The bartenders may be too bored to serve you (oh, the ennui of it all), but during the week the crowd is international and approachable. Don't bother on weekends, when a self-conscious suburbanite crowd takes over.

Where the girls are... Though it thrived during the twenties, when American expats like Djuna Barnes and Natalie Barney lived on the Left Bank, the lesbian scene in Paris today is rather quiet and decidedly more lipstick than leather. There are signs that things are picking up a bit, however, since the popular **El Scandalo** bar opened near the Bastille. The tone here recalls New York's Lower East Side, with the bar hosting art exhibits. The crowd runs from Doc Martens and overalls to models with navel rings in Jean-Paul Gaultier; leave your J. Crew duds at home. Don't be puzzled to see a few men at the front end of **La Champmesle**, since the all-women area is in back. This is Paris's all-purpose lesbian bar, which means that the clientele runs from middle-aged career women in imitation Chanel suits to cyber-chicks with nose rings. The cosmeticized feminine model prevails and dominates the crowd in its busy after-work hours. During the week, it's often rather quiet here late at night, but come the weekend, the place really gets packed.

PARIS ☾ THE BAR SCENE

The Index

L'Académie de la Bière. It's Beer U. at this bar with more than 150 brands from remote corners of the planet.... *Tel 43 54 66 65; 88 bis, bd. Port-Royal, 75005; Métro Port-Royal RER. Closed Sun.*

Amnesia. A Marais gay bar that welcomes men and women.... *Tel 42 72 16 94; 42, rue Vieille-du-Temple, 75004; Métro Hôtel-de-Ville. Open daily.*

Angel Cafe. Near Les Halles, this cafe serves food and drinks until 2am to a mixed crowd that grooves on techno tunes.... *Tel 40 26 28 60; 22, rue Pierre Lescot, 75001; Métro Etienne Marcel. Open daily.*

L'Art Brut. A distressed, artsy facade and interior, and a menu of cheap drinks, make this an ideal place to come if you're planning to invent a new school of philosophy.... *Tel 42 78 18 65; 78, rue Quincampoix 75003; Métro Rambuteau. Closed Sun.*

Banana Café. Mayhem reigns on the weekend in this Les Halles gay cafe-bar replete with go-go dancing boys and a crowd heavy on the drag queens.... *Tel 42 33 35 31; 13, rue de la Ferronerie, 75001; Métro Les Halles. Open daily.*

Le Bar. First-rate jazz, a cool crowd, and well-mixed drinks are worth the cover charge, especially when compared to the very expensive, sadly soulless, tourist jazz holes in the nearby rue Saint-Benoit.... *Tel 43 26 60 00; Hôtel Villa, 29, rue Jacob, 75006; Métro Saint-Germain-des-Prés. Open daily. Music Mon–Fri, 125F cover Mon–Thur, 150F Fri, Sat.*

Bar Belge. More than 50 Belgian beers are available in this bar near the mondo flea market near Porte de Clignancourt.... *Tel 46 27 41 01; 75, av. de Saint-Ouen, 75017; Métro Guy-Môquet. Open daily.*

Bar des Ferailleurs. One of the hippest bars in Paris in one of the coolest parts of town attracts a young, fashion-conscious crowd. Think Jean-Paul Gaultier, not Giorgio Armani. A good post-dinner, pre-club hangout, because the club plays techno and trance music.... *Tel 48 07 89 12; 18, rue de Lappe, 75011; Métro Bastille. Open daily.*

Le Bar Dix. Imbued with Flower Power ambience, this laid-back bar is populated with aging French hippies and other earnest types interested in saving the world and guzzling house sangria.... *Tel 43 26 66 83; 10, rue de l'Odéon, 75006; Métro Odéon. Open daily.*

Le Bar du Palmier. One of the city's largest gay bars, devoid of decor charm, but popular and crowded, especially on weekends.... *Tel 40 41 00 10; 5, rue de la Ferronerie, 75001; Métro Châtelet. Open daily.*

Barfly. Reservations are mandatory in this club that caters to the well-heeled and well-coiffed.... *Tel 53 67 84 60; 49, av. George V, 75008; Métro Alma-Marceau. Open daily.*

Le Barretto. The overstuffed leather chairs and banquettes make this a comfy destination at the end of a day of strolling the Champs-Elysées. Etched glass and discreet lighting create an Italianate mood with art deco overtones. Good Italian wines served by the glass.... *Tel 40 75 04 39; Hôtel de Vigny; 9, rue Balzac, 75008; Métro George-V. Open daily.*

Le Bar Sans Nom. A hip stop in the Bastille, with a beer-drinking, arty crowd and a roomful of mismatched, shabby armchairs. Music ranges from funk to reggae.... *Tel 48 05 59 36; 49, rue de Lappe, 75011; Métro Bastille. Open daily.*

Bar Vendôme. An intimate bar where you can satisfy your curiosity about the legendary Ritz, even if you're not staying here. The stiff prices notwithstanding, this bar looks out on the hotel's pretty interior garden and is a very *soigné* place to tipple and star-spot.... *Tel 43 16 30 30; Hôtel Ritz; 15, place Vendôme, 75001; Métro Concorde. Open daily.*

Le Belier. Intimate, romantic and expensive, this hotel bar is decorated in a theatrical over-the-top style that stops just short of being camp. The small bar, where a pianist holds forth most nights, is a favorite hangout for celebrities with carefully crafted low-key public images—think Keanu Reeves and Faye Dunaway.... *Tel 43 25 27 22; L'Hôtel; 13, rue des Beaux-Arts, 75006; Métro Saint-Germain-des-Prés. Open daily.*

Le Birdland. A charming hole-in-the-wall with a superb collection of jazz records and tapes. Some of the most interesting insomniacs in Paris—appreciative of the gentle lighting—are found here in the wee hours.... *Tel 43 26 97 59; 20, rue Princesse, 75006; Métro Mabillon. Open daily.*

Café Beaubourg. A lively cafe with postmodern decor à la Philippe Starck; a great place to people-watch from behind your omelet.... *Tel 48 87 89 98; 100, rue Saint-Martin, 75004; Métro Châtelet. Open daily.*

Café de Flore. One of the city's best-known cafes, made famous by Jean-Paul Sartre and Simone de Beauvoir. It's still a must for a late-night coffee, cordial, or ice cream.... *Tel 45 48 55 26; 172, bd. Saint-Germain, 75006; Métro Saint-Germain-des-Prés. Open daily.*

Café de la Mairie. Students, book editors, film people, and boutique owners people this much-loved cafe across from place Saint-Sulpice.... *Tel 43 26 67 82; 8 pl. Saint-Sulpice, 75006; Métro Saint-Sulpice. Closed Sun except in June.*

Le Café du Passage. The jazz-cool annex of the Passage restaurant is a happening place to spend a night sniffing corks. Browse the fine selection of wines—note the Chinon and the Crozes-Hermitage. Sip as well as sup on the good salads and light dishes to your heart's content, or at least until 2am.... *Tel 49 29 97 64; 12 rue de Charonne, 75011; Métro Bastille. Closed Sun.*

Café L'Industrie. A cozy, funky cafe in the midst of the trendier-than-thou Bastille. Heavy on atmosphere, light on attitude. Drinks and light food.... *Tel 47 00 13 53; 16, rue Saint-Sabin, 75011; Métro Bastille. Closed Sat.*

Café Marly. Located in the courtyard of the Louvre, this cafe is aces for a light nosh beneath the flow of the I. M. Pei pyramid.... *Tel 49 26 06 60; 93, rue de Rivoli; 75001. Métro Palais-Royal—Musée du Louvre. Open daily.*

Café Orbital. Business types and street flotsam flock to these two branches of Paris's first online cafe.... *Tel 43 25 76 77; 4, rue du Quatre-Septembre, 75002; Métro Bourse. Closed Sunday. Online time costs 55F an hour. Left Bank: 13, rue de Medicis, 75006; Métro Bourse. Closed Sun.*

Le Central. One of the best places for a debut experience of the Paris gay bar scene, because this Marais bar is small and doesn't put out a lot of attitude.... *Tel 48 87 99 33; 33, rue Vieille-du-Temple, 75004; Métro Hôtel-de-Ville. Open daily.*

La Champmesle. One of the city's most popular lesbian bars, with a clientele that runs the gamut in fashion and age.... *Tel 42 96 85 20; 4, rue Chabanais, 75002; Métro Bourse. Open daily.*

Charly's Bar. Paris's only legitimate after-hours bar for serious club-hoppers. On Saturday and Sunday, it closes at 2am, only to reopen at 6am and serve until noon. Deejays spin deep trance and techno for a lit-up, young, post-club crowd.... *Tel 43 26 61 23; 26, rue de la Parcheminerie, 75005; Métro Saint-Michel. Open daily.*

Chez Richard. In this Marais bar, it's echoes of Barcelona with the decor and a thirtysomething crowd quaffing beers on tap or the bar's speciality—margaritas.... *Tel 42 73 31 65; 37, rue Vieille-du-Temple, 75004; Métro Saint-Paul. Open daily.*

China Club. Just down the street from the new Opéra Bastille at the place de la Bastille, this low-key bar is chic, with an interesting, well-tailored crowd and great cocktails....

Tel 43 43 82 02; 50, rue de Charenton, 75012; Métro Bastille. Open daily.

La Closerie des Lilas. Though it retains its cult status with Hemingway fans, this legendary Montparnasse bar and restaurant is often a disappointment to less literary types. This unself-conscious tourist trap would surely incur Papa's wrath if he were around today.... *Tel 43 26 70 50; 171, bd. du Montparnasse, 75014; Métro Vavin. Open daily.*

Clown Bar. Originally built for the *Cirque d'Hiver* nearby, this funky wine bar can be relied on for good simple food, circus memorabilia, and fashion types.... *Tel 43 55 87 35; 114, rue Amelot, 75011; Métro Filles-de-Calvaire. Closed Sun and part of Aug. No credit cards.*

Club Club. A Pigalle bar that endears with its trash-and-flash decor and attitude. It's in the thick of its Warholian 15 minutes.... *Tel 42 54 38 38; 3, rue Antoine, 75009; Métro Pigalle. Open daily.*

Le Comptoir. A trendy, mixed crowd frequents this chic Les Halles bar that serves tapas. A deejay plugs in Thursday through Saturday.... *Tel 40 26 26 66; 14, rue Vauvilliers, 75001; Métro Les Halles RER. Open daily.*

Connolly's Corner. A Latin Quarter bar popular with English-speaking students, tourists, and expats.... *Tel 43 31 94 22; 12, rue Mirabel, 75005; Métro Censier-Daubenton. Open daily.*

Cox's Café. Net-surf on two computers in this new gay bar that is a welcome addition to the Marais scene. In addition to the usual drinks, the bar serves good espresso and has an excellent white Belgian wheat beer on tap. Cool mixed crowd, and women are welcome.... *Tel 42 72 08 00; 15, rue des Archives, 75004; Métro Hôtel-de-Ville. Open daily.*

Le Dépanneur. An American-style diner open 24 hours and good for drinks if you're dead set on reaching oblivion after clubbing around the Place Pigalle.... *Tel 40 16 40 20; 27, rue Fontaine, 75009; Métro Blanche. Open daily.*

Les Deux Magots. Versace to Cafe de Flore's Armani. In bad weather, try the enclosed sidewalk terrace.... *Tel 45 48 55 25; 170, bd. Saint-Germain, 75006. Métro Saint-Germain-des-Prés. Open daily.*

Doobie's. Paris's beautiful people flock to this exclusive and somewhat snobby club off the Champs-Elysées. Dress to kill and prepare to people-watch from a table—no one stands at the bar.... *Tel 53 76 10 76; 2, rue Robert Etienne, 75008; Métro Franklin-D.-Roosevelt. Open daily.*

Le Duplex. A small, friendly Marais bar with art exhibitions and a young gay crowd.... *Tel 42 72 80 86; 25, rue Michel-le-Comte, 75004; Métro Rambuteau. Open daily.*

Flann O'Brien's. There's often live Gaelic music in the evenings, and the generously long happy hour—6–9pm—draws big crowds with its pints of beer for 25 francs.... *Tel 42 60 13 58; 6, rue Bailleul, 75001; Métro Louvre. Open daily.*

La Fleche d'Or. A huge, offbeat club in an abandoned railway station that attracts an artistic crowd. It's funky, a real trek to get to, sometimes almost empty, but usually a lot of fun.... *Tel 43 72 42 44; 102 bis, rue de Bagnolet, 75020; Métro Alexandre Dumas. Closed Tues.*

Le Forum. This small cocktail salon looks like something a Hollywood set designer might have cooked up to look typically Parisian. The regulars are mostly fortysomething professionals. More than 150 varieties of mixed drinks.... *Tel 42 65 37 86; 4, bd. Malesherbes, 75008; Métro Madeleine. Open daily. No cover.*

Le Fouquet's. Once a haunt for James Joyce, now frequented by the global rich, and priced accordingly.... *Tel 47 23 70 60; 99, av. des Champs-Elysées, 75008; Métro George-V. Open daily.*

The Frog and Rosbif. A lively English pub near Les Halles, with a micro-brewery, pub grub, and thick crowds on nights when soccer matches are televised.... *Tel 42 36 34 73; 116, rue Saint-Denis, 75002; Métro Etienne Marcel. Open daily.*

Au General Lafayette. Lite noshes, Belgian beers, and eager crowds in this bar tucked into a quiet neighborhood.... *Tel 47 70 59 08; 52, rue Lafayette, 75009; Métro Le Péletier. Open daily.*

Harry's New York Bar. This legendary bar—where the Bloody Mary was reputedly invented—is less a place to hang out all night than it is a pleasant, convenient spot for a drink before or after dinner or an event at the nearby Opéra Garnier.... *Tel 42 61 71 14; 5, rue Danou, 75001; Métro Opéra. Open daily.*

Hemingway Bar. This snug little bar buried deep in the Ritz— you have to walk the length of the hotel through a long corridor of glass cases baited with luxury goods—was recently renovated in honor of the swashbuckling author, who was one of the first clients to belly up to the bar after the liberation of Paris.... *Tel 43 16 30 30; Hôtel Ritz; 15, place Vendôme, 75001; Métro Concorde. Open daily.*

Hôtel Normandy. A vaguely louche atmosphere and a great location right in the heart of the city—it's only a few steps from the Louvre, if you feel a sudden desire for a respite after seven rooms of Flemish portraits—make this bar sort of an insider's refuge.... *Tel 42 60 30 21; Hôtel Normandy; 7, rue Echelle, 75001; Métro Louvre-Rivoli. Open daily.*

Jacques Melac. It's easy to get happy at this laid-back place with a very high-quality selection of regional French bottles. The Côte du Rhones are especially good, and it's likely that Melac himself will insist that you try a glass of his latest find, on the house. He's that too-rare type of proprietor who wants everyone to discover what he loves.... *Tel 43 70 59 27; 42, rue Leon-Frot, 75001; Métro Charonne. Closed Sat, Sun, Mon nights.*

The James Joyce. An out-of-the-way Irish pub decorated with Joyce memorabilia and serving standard Irish fare.... *Tel 44 09 70 32; 71, bd. Gouvion-Saint-Cyr, 75017; Métro Porte Maillot. Open daily.*

Jip's. In this Les Halles bar the crowd downs *Punch d'Amour,* or Love Punch, a heady rum concoction, and boogies to salsa and fusion jazz.... *Tel 42 33 00 11; 41, rue Saint-Denis, 75001; Métro Les Halles RER. Open daily.*

Juveniles. This British-style wine bar is a good bet for an interesting bottle. In addition to various cold plates, there are incredible tapas, as well as rare French wines you can't easily find at home, and an intriguing selection of foreign wines by the glass. Decorous, professional crowd.... *Tel 42 97 46 49; 47, rue Richelieu, 75001; Métro Palais-Royal-Musée du Louvre. Closed Sun.*

Kitty O'Shea's. A favorite hangout of foreign yuppies drawn to its menu to Irish dishes and brews.... *Tel 40 15 00 30; 10, rue des Capucines, 75002; Métro Opéra. Open daily.*

Le Leche-Vin. A hoot before heading out to a club, this place is a shrine to high camp, with a wacked-out decor of St.-Anthony-on-the-dashboard-style religious art. Lively and fun, the crowd's mixed and more interested in having a good time than wielding heavy attitude.... *Tel 43 55 98 91; 13, rue Daval, 75012; Métro Bastille. Open daily.*

Lili La Tigresse. This bar perpetuates the bump-and-grind traditions of the Pigalle neighborhood with a postmodern spin. The decor is outrageously bordello plush, with velvet and lavish amounts of gilt. Go-go girls, and sometimes boys, shake their stuff on the bar nightly.... *Tel 48 74 08 25; 98, rue Blanche, 75009; Métro Blanche. Closed Sun.*

The Lizard Lounge. A hip, singles place with great decor. A basement bar with a pool table, house music, and an atmosphere agreeable to hanging out all night.... *Tel 42 72 81 34; 18, rue du Bourg-Tibourg, 75004; Métro Hôtel-de-Ville. Open daily.*

Lou Pascalou. A friendly student bar with ultra-cheap drinks; a bottled Heineken goes for about $3, a blow-away bargain for Paris.... *Tel 46 36 78 10; 14, rue des Panoyaux, 75020. Métro Ménilmontant. Open daily.*

Merle Mocquer. An off-the-beaten-path bar in the Butte-aux-Cailles neighborhood of the Left Bank's 13th arrondisement. It's a mellow place to catch the latest French bands and drink cheap beer with a diverse, down-to-earth crowd.... *Tel*

*45 65 12 43; 11, rue de la Butte-aux-Cailles, 75013;
Métro Corvisart. Open daily.*

Ministry. You won't like this place unless you're a serious
heavy-metal fan, but if this is the case you'll probably
groove to the tunes and the mock-dungeon decor.... *Tel
42 82 08 88; 1, rue Mansart, 75009; Métro Blanche.
Open daily.*

Molly Malone's. A lively Irish pub near the Madeleine, with
live music and a casual atmosphere.... *Tel 47 42 07 77;
21, rue Godot de Mauroy, 75009; Métro Madeleine.
Open daily.*

Le Moloko. A Pigalle bar with a Saturday night striptease, a
stocked jukebox, and a postage stamp-size dance floor....
*Tel 48 74 50 26; 26, rue Fontaine, 75009; Métro
Blanche. Open daily. 30F cover on Sat night.*

Montalembert Bar. This is one of the rare hotel bars that
might tempt you to actually settle in with a book. The
spare but attractive decor by fashionable interior designer
Christian Liagre works just as well at night as it does during the day in this bar frequented by stylish Left Bank
types.... *Tel 45 48 68 11; 3, rue Montalembert, 75007;
Métro Rue du Bac.*

Le 9. Almost everyone feels comfortable in this Ile St.-Louis
bar—middle-aged professional couples, club kids, two
females traveling together. The restaurant serves French
classics, and a bar and a club with a pool table are downstairs.... *Tel 44 07 22 74; 5–9, rue Bude, 75004; Métro
Pont-Neuf. Open daily until 6am.*

Oscar Wilde. The crowd in this Les Halles bar ranges from a
mixed bag of young French tourists to Anglophile expats....
*Tel 42 21 03 63; 38, rue Bourdonnais, 75001; Métro Les
Halles RER. Open daily.*

Oz Cafe. Australian-themed bar with Down Under beer and
wine; frequented by expat Aussies, Yanks, and Brits. The
rock soundtrack features breaking bands from Down Under.
Many people prefer the Latin Quarter original to its new
branch in Les Halles—they say the former is more inti-

mate.... *Tel 43 54 30 48; 184, rue Saint-Jacques, 75005; Métro Luxembourg RER. Open daily. In Les Halles: Tel 40 39 00 18; 18, rue Saint-Denis, 75002; Métro Châtelet RER. Open daily.*

La Palette. An authentic art-nouveau cafe, popular with Beaux-Arts students and antique and art dealers.... *Tel 43 26 68 15; 43, rue de Seine, 75006; Métro Mabillon. Closed Sun.*

Pandora Station. This Pigalle bar is another post-club venue with a fabulous mix of demimonde types who love to play until the wee hours.... *Tel 45 26 24 11; 24, rue Fontaine, 75009; Métro Pigalle. Open daily.*

Pause Café. A low-key cafe, strategically located for nighttime drop-ins or just watching the hipsters pass by.... *Tel 48 06 80 33; 41, rue de Charonne, 75011; Métro Ledru-Rollin. Open daily.*

La Perla. This attractive, low-key, Mexican-style cantina in the Marais does an honorable job of mixing the city's meanest margaritas. The bar also serves beer and Mexican food, and draws an attractive, stylish crowd of all ages.... *Tel 42 77 59 40; 26, rue Francois-Miron, 75004; Métro Saint-Paul. Open daily.*

Le Petit Fer à Cheval. A convivial Marais bar with an authentic Parisian feel and an atmosphere conducive to conversation.... *Tel 42 72 47 47; 30, rue Vieille-du-Temple; Métro Saint-Paul. Open daily.*

Le Piano Vache. A classic student bar in charmingly frayed surroundings.... *Tel 46 33 75 03; 8, rue Laplace, 75005; Métro Maubert-Mutualité. Open daily.*

Le Piano Zinc. Three levels of gay, campy fun, with live performances in the basement and a pianist.... *Tel 42 74 32 42; 49, rue-des-Blancs-Manteaux, 75004; Métro Hôtel-de-Ville. Closed Mon. 45F cover, including one drink.*

Le Pick-Clops. This raucous joint is a good bet for anyone who wants an alternative to the more restrained chic of other Marais bars. This authentic neighborhood bar predates the

PARIS ☾ THE BAR SCENE

area's gentrification, and though the neon lighting flatters no one, the wattage is filtered through thick clouds of cigarette smoke.... *Tel 40 29 02 18; 16, rue Vieille-du-Temple, 75004; Métro Hôtel-de-Ville. Open daily.*

Polly Magoo's. A collegiate, nostalgic bar popular with Sorbonne students past and present.... *Tel 46 33 33 64; 11, rue Saint-Jacques, 75003; Métro Cluny-La-Sorbonne. Open daily.*

La Poste. A basement bar in the restaurant housed in a 19th-century mansion. This Pigalle bar is quiet and stylish and peopled with French media and movie types.... *Tel 45 26 50 00; 22, rue de Douai, 75009; Métro Place de Clichy. Open daily.*

Pub Saint-Germain. Sometimes there's a whiff of frat-house frolics in the air at this rollicking anchor of Left Bank nightlife, but because the place is so enormous, you can always find a quieter corner if your mood is more sedate.... *Tel 43 29 38 70; 17, rue de l'Ancienne-Comédie, 75006; Métro Odéon. Open daily 24 hours.*

Pub 64 WE. If you really don't want to surf the scene in the trendier places around the Bastille, but still hope to hang out with a cool crowd, this is a relaxed place to spend some time. Two pool tables, a friendly, often bilingual crowd of interesting regulars, and an appealing drinks list, including several bottled Czech beers, Belgian Kriek (flavored with cherries), and Dame Blanche on tap.... *Tel 44 75 39 55; 64, rue de Charenton, 75012; Métro Ledru-Rollin. Open daily.*

Le Quetzal. This gay bar is small and amiable and mobbed on Sunday afternoons.... *Tel 48 87 99 07; 10, rue de la Verrerie, 75004; Métro Hôtel-de-Ville. Open daily.*

Quigley's Point. Irish bartenders serve in this authentic pub. On a rainy day, come in for a game of pool or to watch the Sky sports channel. The sidewalk terrace is a draw during the summer.... *Tel 45 08 17 04; 5, rue du Jour, 75001; Métro Les Halles RER. Open daily.*

Le Reservoir. The mood is vaguely Tarantino at this super-cool cafe-bar-restaurant near the Bastille. The food isn't the draw here; it's the excellent table-hopping crowd.... *Tel 43 56 39 60; 16, rue de la Forge-Royale, 75011; Metro Ledru-Rollin. Open daily.*

Le Rosebud. A pleasant and entertaining place for an after-dinner drink, some hand-holding, and a *prélude d'amour*.... *Tel 43 35 38 54; 11 bis, rue Delambre, 75014; Métro Vavin. Open daily.*

Le Rubis. A relaxed and unpretentious traditional wine bar. Very popular after-work meeting place, famed for its annual Beaujolais nouveau fête.... *Tel 42 61 03 34; 10, rue du Marche-Saint-Honoré, 75001; Métro Tuileries. Closed Sat night, Sun.*

Le Sancerre. People-watching and Pernod-sipping on a front terrace of this cafe with an arty crowd.... *Tel 42 58 08 20; 35, rue des Abbesses, 75018; Métro Abbesses. Open daily.*

Sanz Sans. A very popular Bastille bar with bordello decor, a hip crowd, and throngs of suburbanites on the weekends.... *Tel 44 75 78 78; 49, rue du Faubourg Saint-Antoine, 75012; Métro Bastille. Open daily.*

Le Satellit Café. Proof that a club-bar can be truly cool without packing a nasty attitude, this friendly, comfortable place guarantees a good night out, especially for oenophiles and fans of ethnic music. The deejay mixes Algerian *rai* with tunes from the West Indies, Zaire, Madagascar, and Egypt.... *Tel 47 00 48 87; 44, rue de la Folie Mericourt, 75011; Métro Oberkampf. Open daily.*

El Scandalo. Just about the only place for a cool, worldly gal to go if she wants to meet like-minded ladies.... *Tel 47 00 24 59; 24, rue Keller, 75011; Métro Bastille. Open daily.*

Le Select. This Montparnasse bar flourished during the twenties and thirties and retains authentic decor and ambience.... *Tel 42 22 65 27; 99, bd. du Montparnasse, 75006; Métro Vavin. Open daily.*

Le Sous-Bock Tavern. It's beer here, with more than 400 in stock, including 12 on tap, at this friendly bar.... *Tel 40 26*

46 61; 49, rue Saint-Honoré, 75001; Métro Châtelet. Open daily.

Stolly's. A popular, tiny Marais bar with affordable beer and an amiable, English-speaking clientele.... *Tel 42 76 06 76; 16, rue Cloche-Perce, 75004; Métro Hôtel-de-Ville. Open daily.*

La Tartine. Raise a glass of white Sancerre to Trotsky at this charmingly proletariat, old wine bar in the heart of the Marais. A politely subversive mood thrives in slightly shabby surroundings. The name means an open-face sandwich, and the bar serves a large variety of same. Ideal for a sip and a snack in the Marais before moving on to someplace more nocturnal; the bar closes at 10pm.... *Tel 42 72 76 85; 24, rue de Rivoli, 75004; Métro Hôtel-de-Ville. Closed Tues, Wed morning.*

La Taverne Phify's. The ultimate French biker-bar. Phify himself is quite a critter—an avid biker, former rock star, and bodyguard. He's on the premises most evenings, greeting the bikers and their babes. More of a Levi's than a Calvin Klein place.... *Tel 47 00 78 44; 74, rue de la Roquette, 75011; Métro Bastille. Open daily.*

Le Trap. The only remaining gay bar in Saint-Germain-des-Prés.... *Tel 43 54 53 53; 10, rue Jacob, 75006; Métro Saint-Germain-des-Prés. Open daily.*

Le Violon Gingue. A Latin Quarter student bar with cheap beer and twentysomethings looking for love in all the wrong places.... *Tel 43 31 78 77; 46, rue de la Montagne-Sainte-Genevieve, 75005; Métro Maubert-Mutualité. Open daily.*

Web Bar. A Marais online cafe where the patrons wear black and jazz bubbles in the background.... *Tel 42 72 66 55; 32, rue de Picardie, 75002; Métro Filles du Calvaire. Open daily. Online charge is 50F an hour.*

What's Up Bar. This Bastille bar is *the* stop if you're willing to take attitude right in the face and listen to the city's best club deejay-spun music with the likes of designers, models, musicians, and the haute hot of Paris.... *Tel 48 05 88 33; 11, rue Daval, 75011; Métro Bastille. Open daily.*

Willi's Wine Bar. A sophisticated crowd of regulars comes here to get at one of the best by-the-glass offers in Paris. The crowd's worldly and friendly, and you can also get an appealing light meal here—maybe a slice of paté and a bit of salad.... *Tel 42 61 05 09; 13, rue des Petits-Champs, 75001; Métro Pyramides. Closed Sun.*

Le Zephyr. Near Le Palace, this cafe is a piece of authentic Paris in the midst of fast-food franchise mania.... *Tel 47 70 80 14; 12, bd. Montmartre, 75009; Métro Rue Montmartre. Open daily.*

Zowezo. A cyber-cafe that plays salsa and reggae tunes and attracts an odd and interesting mixture of people.... *Tel 40 23 00 71; 37, rue Fontaine, 75009; Métro Blanche. Closed Monday. Online charge is 50F an hour.*

Central Paris Bars

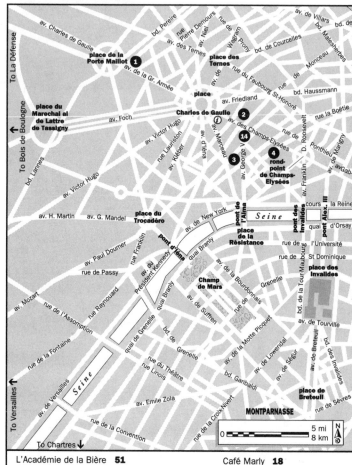

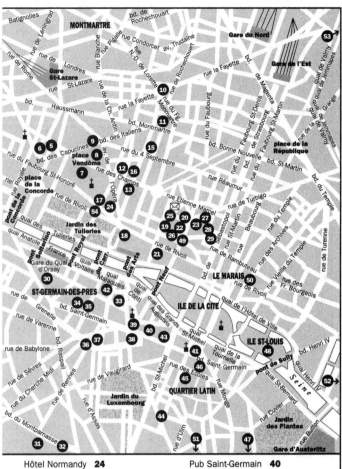

Hôtel Normandy **24**	Pub Saint-Germain **40**
The James Joyce **1**	Quigley's Point **25**
Jip's **27**	Le Rosebud **31**
Juvenile's **12**	Le Rubis **54**
Kitty O'Shea's **9**	Sanz Sans **52**
Lou Pascalou **53**	Le Satellit Cafe **52**
Merle Mocquer **47**	El Scandalo **52**
Molly Malone's **5**	Le Select **32**
Montalembert Bar **30**	Le Sous-Bock Tavern **49**
Le 9 **48**	La Tartine **50**
Oscar Wilde **26**	La Taverne Phify's **52**
Oz Cafe **44**	Le Trap **33**
La Palette **39**	Le Violon Gingue **45**
Le Piano Vache **46**	Willi's Wine Bar **13**
Polly Magoo's **41**	Le Zephyr **11**

Montmartre Bars

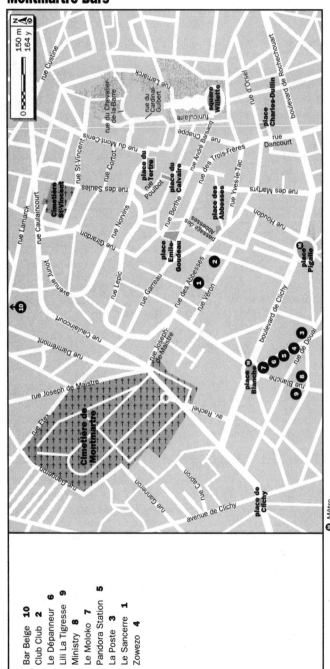

Bar Belge **10**
Club Club **2**
Le Dépanneur **6**
Lili La Tigresse **9**
Ministry **8**
Le Moloko **7**
Pandora Station **5**
La Poste **3**
Le Sancerre **1**
Zowezo **4**

M Métro

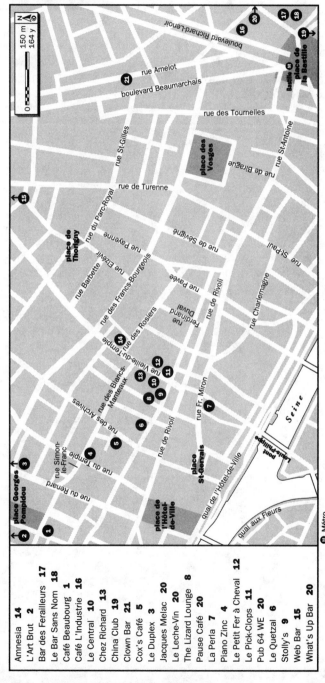

The Marais Bars

Amnesia **14**
L'Art Brut **2**
Bar des Ferailleurs **17**
Le Bar Sans Nom **18**
Café Beaubourg **1**
Café L'Industrie **16**
Le Central **10**
Chez Richard **13**
China Club **19**
Clown Bar **21**
Cox's Café **5**
Le Duplex **3**
Jacques Melac **20**
Le Leche-Vin **20**
The Lizard Lounge **8**
Pause Café **20**
La Perla **7**
Piano Zinc **4**
Le Petit Fer à Cheval **12**
Le Pick-Clops **11**
Pub 64 WE **20**
Le Quetzal **6**
Stolly's **9**
Web Bar **15**
What's Up Bar **20**

the

arts

3

Long considered one of
the great cultural capitals
of the Western world,
Paris offers an endless,
high-caloric feast of music,
opera, theater, and dance.
During his long reign,

the late President François Mitterand showered money on arts groups and organizations as generously as the U.S. government funds the Pentagon. But as it turns out, fat budgets alone don't induce creativity. In spite of the lavish state subsidies, you're more often likely to find innovative programming in Boston or Barcelona than you are in the French capital. To make things worse, despite Mitterand's original intentions to turn art into a staple of the French daily diet, with such projects as the ghastly Opéra Bastille (supposedly the "people's opera house," as opposed to the allegedly effete Palais Garnier), it never occurred to anyone that the fastest and best way to draw audiences to dance, music, and opera might be to lower ticket prices. Depending on the event, decent seats at the Opéra Bastille average $80 a ticket and must be reserved well in advance.

As for the stage, *si vous parlez français,* you'll have the pick of the city's vast theatrical offerings; Paris has the largest number of theaters of any urban center in the world. If you don't know what *si vous parlez français* means, though, you're probably limited to English-language theater, of which there's not a wealth here. It's generally best to ignore the commercial theater, which runs to miserable versions of Broadway and the West End, in favor of the excellent classical or serious contemporary productions, usually state-subsidized, that are offered at the **Comédie Française**, effectively the French national theater, the **Odéon Théâtre de l'Europe**, or the **Théâtre National de Chaillot**.

The city's music scene is in a fevered period of activity. Government money has built first-rate music halls. Paris is home to three major symphony orchestras and is a usual stop for touring orchestras from the United States and Europe. Opera continues to thrive and opera fans are gaga over **Roberto Alagna**, a 31-year-old opera sensation. The music menu in the city is always full, but the most noteworthy item these days is contemporary music, particularly rap and world music, thanks to large populations from West Africa, the Caribbean, and Latin America, with French stars like **M.C. Solaar** and **Ethnique Alliance**. New venues for contemporary music include the just-completed **Cité de la Musique** and **IRCAM**, a music research institute founded by Pierre Boulez, acknowledged as France's greatest living composer.

To scope out what's on and what's coming, Paris has several magazines: ***Pariscope***, ***L'Officiel des Spectacles***, and ***Sept à Paris***. All are published on Wednesdays and are available at citywide newsstands. *Boulevard* is a bimonthly magazine published in English, and includes cultural events listings.

Getting Tickets

Most box offices open daily at 11am and accept credit card reservations by phone. But arrive at least an hour early to pick up your tickets, or some box offices will sell them to someone else. If you're really desperate to go to the opera, see a specific play, or attend a concert of a particular group or artist, it's worth calling in advance to reserve your tickets. The **Kiosque Théâtre**, with two branches at the Place de la Madeleine and in front of the Gare Montparnasse, offers same-day, half-price theater tickets, so check with them first if there's a play that interests you. Credit cards are not accepted at Kiosque. (Also note that if your cheapo tickets are marked *sans visibilité* you won't be able to see the stage). Other ticket outlets are the **Virgin Megastore** and **FNAC**, a citywide chain of book and music stores, a sort of French Ticketmaster with tickets for most of the city's cultural events. Another, more costly option is **Specta Plus**, a commercial booking agency that charges a variable but generally rather stiff commission for tickets. Still, if you're desperate to attend something, they accept bookings and credit card charges by phone and can usually find you a seat (tel 43 59 39 39, fax 45 63 56 26; closed Sun). If that fails, or your budget doesn't let you go to a ticket broker, stand in front of the venue with a sign that says *cherche une place* and try your luck.

The Lowdown

Where it's at... The most exciting event in French music circles in years was the opening of the **Cité de la Musique**. This new music center in a white-stone pie wedge of a building complex by Pritzker-prizewinning architect Christian de Portzamparc (who also designed the popular Café Beaubourg next to the Centre Pompidou) is the last major component of the Parc de la Villette, a 40-acre urban-renewal project on the site of the former municipal slaughterhouses in the 19th arrondissement on the northwest edge of the city. Its west wing, the Cité Oeust, houses the National Music and Dance Conservatory; the Cité Est, on the eastern corner, includes a 1200-seat concert hall, a smaller 230-seat amphitheater, rehearsal halls, a video-interactive library and documentation center, a laboratory for the restoration of musical instruments, and the headquarters of the Ensemble Intercontemporain, founded by composer extraordinaire Pierre Boulez, to promote contemporary music. Though the unchallenged wisdom is that Paris is among the top three cities in the world—with London and New York—for classical music, Boulez recently gave everyone a shock when he savaged the city's reputation as a music center during an interview on the occasion of his seventieth birthday. When asked whether Paris is a capital of music, he said, "No! And I don't think it has been one for a very long time. This is just a myth. In 1840, during a trip, Wagner said that he'd never heard Beethoven's symphonies better played anywhere in the world than Paris. Do you think a composer of this level could say the same thing today? No! There's too much dilettantism here. The professional level of the city's musical life is not very high." Though most music lovers would find Boulez's judgment too severe, it is true that the enormous amount of public money made available for classical music has somewhat insulated the Parisian community from the inconvenient necessity of producing programs people actually want to hear. Still, Paris has extraordinary music in a brilliant variety of settings, beginning with the prestigious **Salle Pleyel**, the single most important venue for classical concerts and the home of the Orchestre de Paris. It's named after composer and pianomaker Ignace Pleyel. As a space, it's not particularly remarkable; the acoustics are acceptable, but the hall lacks atmosphere and doesn't always work very well. More charming is the **Salle Gaveau**, a delightful place named after the firm of renowned French pianomakers. This hall is best for piano recitals and chamber music. The **Maison de Radio France**, the single largest radio-broadcasting installation in the world, is also a very interesting place to attend a concert. The main concert hall here is the Salle Olivier Messiaen, where the programming varies widely. Other primary venues include the **Châtelet** (or **Théâtre Musical de Paris**, as it is also called), the **Opéra Bastille**, the **Théâtre des Champs-Elysées**, the **Opéra Comique–Salle Favart**, and the **Palais Garnier**.

Figaro, Figaro, Figaro... Parisians are avid operagoers, and the Paris opera season draws real worldwide aficionados. Maybe it's because opera stirs the Latin soul in a way that people from non-Mediterranean countries can't quite understand, or perhaps it's because the formality, elegance, and discipline of the operagoing experience corresponds so ideally to the apotheosis of refinement that is at the core of all performing arts events in Paris. Then, too, any situation that favors intricate social coding suits Parisians to a T. Because opera is popular, you should book your tickets well in advance. Paris has been aflutter over the emergence of the first major, new French opera star in a long time—tenor Roberto Alagna. Alagna, a 31-year-old Frenchman of Sicilian parents, who started out as a singing waiter (before winning a voice competition), currently sings with the **Opéra Bastille** and recently enjoyed a roaring success at the Opéra de Lyon, where he sang Donizetti's *L'elisir d'amore.*

One way or another, the city has a generally superb opera menu, and a night at the **Palais Garnier** represents the quintessence of an *haute-bourgeois* cultural experience. The renovation of the Palais Garnier has been a key event in the Paris opera scene. The gorgeous, gilt palace in the heart of the city was once the capital's main opera house. Following a complete overhaul of its main theater (renovations will continue until the year 2000), the 1875 vintage building commissioned by Emperor Napoleon III is not only more glamorous and beautiful than it has been in years, but also as technically up-to-date as the **Opéra Bastille**, the city's other major performing arts venue. The Bastille is a bit of a letdown in the same way that the Metropolitan Opera in New York is for Europeans; despite all the money lavished on it and its prominence on the city's cultural landscape, it lacks a certain aesthetic rigor and fails to elicit the corresponding social response to high culture that Parisians so relish. Curiously, however, the best recent opera performances have not taken place at either of the Paris operas but at the **Châtelet**, known also as the **Théâtre Musical de Paris**. Recent highlights here have included fine productions of *Peter Grimes; King Arthur, the English Worthy,* and *Wozzeck,* which was conducted by Daniel Barenboim, former director of the Opéra Bastille. **Peniche Opéra**, set on a barge in the Canal Saint Martin, also has an appealing program of vocal music.

Orchestras... Paris is splendidly endowed with orchestras (the city houses three major ones), ranging from the excellent Orchestre Philharmonique, based at the Maison de Radio France, to the Ensemble Orchestral de Paris and the Orchestre National de France. Perhaps the most innovative orchestra is the Orchestre Symphonique Français, a young group that specializes in mostly 19th-century music and makes a noble effort to keep its prices down. It's based at the Maison de Radio France and also plays at the **Théâtre des Champs-Elysées**. This company was invigorated by the arrival of new director Charles Dutoit in 1991. Local consensus has it that this orchestra had been drifting during the tenure of former director Lorin Maazel, but that its programming and performances have improved vastly during the last few years. Audiences here are broader and more varied than they are at some of the other orchestras, and are often drawn by visiting stars such as Yo Yo Ma. The Orchestre Philharmonique, which plays at the Maison de Radio France and the **Salle Pleyel**, is considered by many demanding classical music aficionados to be the finest orchestra in Paris, so if you have only the time or resources for a single classical concert, this is the group to see. Director Marek Janowski is a demanding professional, and this company often plays otherwise neglected French music. Jean-Jacques Kantorow, the new musical director of the Ensemble Orchestral de Paris (which plays at the Salle Pleyel), has enlivened their programming with with works by such twentieth-century mainstays as Copland, Ives, and Kordaly. The Orchestre National de Paris is the most popular French orchestra and plays at the Salle Pleyel or the **Châtelet–Théâtre Musical de Paris**. Under the direction of Semyon Bychkov, who took over after Daniel Barenboim departed to briefly run the Opéra Bastille, its programming became more traditional as Bychkov tried to steer the company back to a classic French orchestral sound and style. In June 1996, however, the baton was passed on to Georges-François Hirsch. A delightful expression of the French love of music is the Fête de la Musique, an annual event generally held in the third week of June, when then there are free concerts all over France.

Go for baroque... Lovers of the baroque will want to make a pilgrimage to the new **Cité de la Musique** at la Villette on the northeastern edge of Paris. Within this rather grand new complex, there's a fascinating just-opened Musée de la Musique, with 4,500 musical instruments from the 16th century to the present and an aural tour of the history of music. Musical offerings range from French baroque opera to jazz. Les Arts Florissant, led by American William Christie, who is a 22-year Paris resident and is widely acknowledged (even by the French) to be the master of French

PARIS ⟨ THE ARTS

baroque music, played at the opening of La Cité de la Musique. The group usually performs its program of composers such as Rameau and Lully at the **Châtelet–Théâtre Musical de Paris**. If they're performing while you're in town, you should pounce on tickets immediately.

Pew music... Some of the most wonderful concerts in town—not surprisingly, often featuring organ music— are held in various churches around Paris. A church concert allows you to do a bit of easygoing sightseeing at the same time you're enjoying the tunes. Programs run to Mozart, Handel, Haydn, Brahms, and company, and the general quality of these performances, some of which are free, is exceptional. Church concerts are also a particularly good bet during the summer, especially in August when the musical season is at its annual ebb. Two of the best organs in the city are found at the **Cathédral de Notre-Dame** and the **Eglise Saint-Eustache** on the edge of Les Halles. **La Madeleine** is often the venue for choral concerts, while the experience of a concert at **Saint-Chapelle**, with its magnificent stained glass windows, is almost other-worldly magical. Other historic churches with music offerings include **St-Julien-le-Pauvre**, a charming medieval church on the edge of the Latin Quarter; **St-Germain-des-Prés**, the old abbey church in the heart of Saint Germain; and **St-Louis-en-L'Ile**, a delightful baroque church that often has baroque programs. For general information about free church concerts, call 40 30 10 13. The Paris Tourist Office at 49 52 53 54 can also give you church concert information, or check their English-language recording at 49 52 53 56.

Music at the museums... Though millions come to the museums of Paris every year to catch a glimpse of the *Mona Lisa* and other artistic treasures, few come to hear music. In fact, many museums in Paris also offer musical programs in their own auditoriums, including the chamber music series at the **Musée du Louvre** and the **Musée d'Orsay**, and occasional charming performances of Renaissance or medieval music at the **Musée de Cluny**. These concerts are usually less expensive than in the major halls, but they're popular, so keep an eye out in the arts listings or when you're wandering around the museum during the daytime.

The dance... The Paris Opéra Ballet, glamorously based at the **Palais Garnier** and brought to world prominence by the late Rudolph Nureyev, remains the ballast of the Paris dance scene and is generally regarded as a first-rate company. Stars to watch for include Laurent Hilaire and Fanny Gaida. Though he now mostly works in the capacity of creative director or choreographer, Patrick Dupont sometimes appears on special occasions. Paris also hosts William Forsyth's Ballet Frankfurt, the New York City Ballet, and a variety of other foreign dance companies every year, and is an important center of contemporary dance as well. Classical choreographer Roland Petit is headquartered in Marseilles, but regularly appears in Paris, as does the Béjart Ballet.

Modern dance... Government money continues to assure the production of a lot of shudderingly awful modern dance all over Paris. A case in point is choreographer Maguy Marin, who's based at the Maison des Arts et de la Culture in Créteil, a rather bleak eastern suburb. You either love her very cerebral and abstract compositions or you loathe them. Suffice it to say that prudence dictates that you bring along a good book if you're going to one of her performances; this way you can avail yourself of the comfortable, well-lit lobby if you find the dance not to your taste. The varying program of the **Théâtre de la Ville** features dancers like the controversial young Flemish performer Jan Fabry and Pina Bausch. Bausch has had a great impact on the style of contemporary French dance; other influences include Japanese *butoh* dance and rap dancing. **Espace Kiron**, though small and simple, is another good place to see modern dance.

Snap, crackle, pop music... Going to a concert in Paris can be a fantastic experience because French audiences often bring out the best in a favorite performer; Aretha Franklin's *Aretha in Paris* remains some of the best singing she ever did, and even Madonna got all juiced up to croon here. Paris is also a good place to catch breaking European artists and groups who haven't made it across the Atlantic yet, and also to feast on local

PARIS ⟨ THE ARTS

talent—Johnny Hallyday, for example. This fiftysome-thing crooner, whose spotted love life has kept the pulp mills churning ever since he first became a star in the early sixties, is a uniquely French phenomenon. Totally unknown outside of the French-speaking world, Johnny is a sort of "Twilight Zone" hybrid of Elvis and Johnny Cash, with a dose of Tom Jones and Liberace thrown in for good measure. And the music? Sort of French coun-try-and-western rock. You've got to see and hear to believe, so if he's performing while you're in town, jump on some tickets. Rap lovers should keep an ear cocked for M.C. Solaar, the star of the scene; IAM, a hot rap group from Marseilles; or Ethnique Alliance, another group from Marseilles which also reflects the enormous ethnic diversity of that city and points toward a new musical hybrid in France, its members' origins ranging from the French West Indies to North Africa. Rap fans accustomed to hard-edged American styles of hip-hop should be warned, though, that the French have put a softer, more comfortable finish on that sound. IRCAM, the center for contemporary music founded by Pierre Boulez, still dominates the modern music scene and receives the lion's share of public monies allotted to new compositions every year; the quality of their output, however, is uneven. **Palais des Congress**, a generally disliked auditorium with the saving grace of good acoustics, and **Elysée Montmartre**, an old music hall, are two oft-used concert venues.

Life is a cabaret... When we think of cabarets, we most likely conjure celluloid images of smoky cafes with patrons huddled around tables. What transformed a cafe into a cabaret was the entertainment. Paris has a long history indeed of showcasing talent in cafes, but these days the venue has changed a bit. The café-théâtres of current times bear scant resemblance to the cafes of yesteryear. For traditional cabaret-style enter-tainment, seek a *chansonnier*, where folk music and bal-lads predominate. *Chansonnier* literally means song writer, though today it is the term for bombastic, ribald musical satire about politics, etiquette, gossip, and the foibles of everyday life. Targets of the humor are often prostitutes, politicians (some say the two are inter-changeable), and the police. Sort of a hybrid burlesque, parody, and dinner theater, chansonniers and the musical satire they have produced have been a staple of Parisian entertainment since days of yore. One of the city's most popular and reliable is at **Le Lapin Agile**. Your French must be in good shape to catch the wordplay and double entendres, and a reasonably strong knowledge of the French political scene will be necessary if you hope to catch the political satire. A cabaret performance by Paris resident (by way of Germany) Ute Lemper at her favorite **Bouffes du Nord** theater—a fantastic place, also much favored by Peter Brook—is completely unforgettable. American DeeDee Bridgewater has lived in Paris for years and is also worth catching.

Big music concert halls... Palais d'Omnisports de **Bercy**, a hideous, troglodyte bunker on the eastern edge of town, has dreadful acoustics but 16,000 seats and usually hosts most of the largest events. More atmospheric are **La Cigale** and the **Elysée Montmartre**, which host diverse billings in medium-size venues. **Le Bataclan** is almost everyone's favorite play date for its Belle Epoque murals, good sight lines and acoustics, and large dance floor. **The Olympia**, with its big, red-neon marquee, has the advantage of a central location near the Madeleine, and continues to exert a mystical hold on Paris concertgoers. Most of the greatest French post-war crooners have appeared here. Jazz fans should also track the monthly concerts held at the **Auditorium du Châtelet**, which offers an innovative program and good acoustics even if the seating is uncomfortable for anyone taller than six feet.

The theatah... Though Paris has the largest number of theaters in the world, your interest will obviously depend upon whether you understand French. If you do, the capital's a fantastic place to catch a classic production of Molière or Racine at the elegant **Comédie Française**. Flanking the Palais Royal, this venerable theater was inaugurated by Louis XIV and has since become the most prestigious stage in the francophone world. A Left Bank branch of the Comédie Française, the **Théâtre du Vieux Colombier**, opened in 1993, and this intimate venue hosts smaller plays and some modern drama. The **Cartoucherie de Vincennes**, a complex

PARIS ⟨ THE ARTS

of five theaters in the Bois de Vincennes, can also be counted on for innovative productions. Before you pack off to a performance by Corneille, however, remember that even if you have a reasonably good command of contemporary French, much of 18th-century *français* could leave you mystified. Be forewarned as well that French theatergoing habits are sometimes rather rigorous, as in a three-hour play with no intermission, so think twice about that cheap seat, especially if you have long legs. This being said, almost anyone can follow a performance by one of the city's great theatrical treasures, the Argentine dramatist and actor Alfredo Arias, whose recent works include a production called *Fausto Argentino,* an antic, campy version of the legend of Faust transposed to an Argentine setting. Paris generally has a respectable offering of serious contemporary French plays, as well as remarkable international theaters like the **Odéon Théâtre de l'Europe**, which is not only a magnificent building but one of the best theaters in Europe and shows a generally superb billing of classic and contemporary European plays, performed in their original language under the auspices of top directors. If you're lucky, you might find a production of *Goldoni* in Italian by a director like Luca Ronconi, or put your German to the test by submitting to a Peter Handke play in the language of Goethe. Similarly, you should check and see if British director Peter Brook, based in the shabby and so wonderfully atmospheric **Bouffes du Nord** theater, has anything on while you're in town. The **Poche Montparnasse**, a pair of small stages, is also a regular venue for serious quality drama. Though its stunning art-deco interior makes it one of the most opulent theaters in Paris, the **Théâtre National de Chaillot** produces mainly crowd pleasers that may or may not be to your taste. After that, in Paris theaterland it's mostly a downhill skid, because the type of musicals and light entertainments that are the bread-and-butter of Broadway and London's West End go all soggy in Paris. If you've seen a British production of Joe Orton, for example, you'll wince at how overacted a French-language version will be, and insofar as musicals are concerned, Broadway hoofers have nothing to worry about from their French compères. So before the curtain goes up in Paris, you're better off going highbrow or you might accidentally end up parked in a seat at something surreally awful, like the smash hit musical *Starmania*, a bizarre *Clockwork Orange* meets *La Cage Aux Folles* mess that inexplicably ran for years, as if everyone were too embarrassed to point out how ghastly it really was.

Café-théâtres... Perfectly fluent doctoral students in search of fringe theater might want to try one of the café-théâtres, a uniquely French institution that usually runs to satirical plays or one-person shows. Two of the best, both in the Marais, are the **Blancs-Manteaux**, with two 100-seat theaters, and the more intimate **Café de la Gare**, where Gérard Depardieu first got his foot in the door.

Theater *en anglais*... The notorious prickliness of the French with regard to the fact that the language of Shakespeare has come to dominate the Western world means that you should stop over in London first if you're looking for English-language theater. The **Théâtre Nesle** in the Latin Quarter is the most interesting, and in truth, the only venue for English-language plays in Paris, and features some of the surprisingly numerous and good anglophone actors and actresses here.

With junior in tow... Though you'll see almost frighteningly well-dressed and behaved children in abundance during the day in parks like the Jardins de Luxembourg—a brilliant place to go with your kids because of the puppet shows, pony rides, and child-friendly snack bars—you very rarely ever see little ones out after about 5pm. Ask Parisians what to do with children at night, and they'll tell you to put them to bed. It's not that Parisians don't like wee ones, but they consider the night to be the province of people old enough to carry credit cards. For a baby-sitter, most hotels can help you out, or call **Inter-Service Parents** (tel 44 93 44 93). If you're going to be in town for a while, check the bulletin board at the American Church, and be prepared for rates averaging $10 an hour. The only museum with late hours that kids might enjoy is the **Musée National d'Histoire Naturelle**, which stays open until 10pm on Thursdays.

PARIS 〜 THE ARTS

For cineastes... Cinema going is the most spontaneous and broadly available cultural activity in Paris, easily the best film city in the world. At any given moment, it seems as though the entire oeuvre of major Western cinema is available somewhere in town, to say nothing of an outstanding selection of European, Asian, African, and Latin American films often excluded by North American distributors. *VO* and *VF* are the key abbreviations to the film listings, meaning *voix originale* and *voix française.* If you don't speak French, you obviously will prefer an English *VO;* you also have to be careful not to head off to the *VF* version of an American or English film; this might lead to the surreal experience of hearing Tom Hanks speaking French in a film like *Forrest Gump.*

For francophones, there's also the wild and wacky world of French cinema. Truth be told, it's more the exception than the rule that the French will be producing anything you want to see these days. Their ferocious cinematographic patriotism to one side, a lot of contemporary French films are bogged down in the same boilerplate plot: Claire loves Guillaume, but she also loves Edouard, who knows nothing of Guillaume. Uh oh, looks like someone's going to end up disguised as a clown or hiding in a closet.

Matthieu Kassovitz is a key exception to this sweeping generalization. The son of Hungarian immigrants, he established himself as the most serious and trenchant of young directors with *La Haine* ("Hate"), an uncompromising film focusing on the alienated working-class youth who live in the projects which surround Paris. Kassovitz is currently the best hope for a new wave of realism in French cinema (e.g., movies with no balloons in them), and someone to spend an evening on if you want to tap into what those Parisians sitting all around you in the darkened theater and fingering their Gauloises are really worried about. There are also French actors and actresses who are worth a sugary situation comedy: Beatrice Dalle has a certain trashy charm, Catherine Deneuve is a brilliant and underrecognized comedienne, as is Josiane Balasko, star of *Gazon Maudit*, a recent smash hit with a bisexual theme—the kind of so-called pink comedy the French have a taste for. And who could remain indifferent to the talents of elegant veteran and *Belle de Jour* star Michel Piccoli, Smain, a comic of North African origins whose popularity sheds some light on the French reverence for Jerry Lewis, or Antoine de Caunes? The latter is currently the coolest of cool French celebrities, a hyphenate (actor-writer, etc.) who also co-hosts a smash hit TV show with Jean-Paul Gaultier out of London, "Eurotrash." Need we say more?

It should also be noted that French cinemas are cleaner and more comfortable than most of their North American counterparts. Note, too, that Monday night is discount night at the movies when the normal price of 45 francs is reduced to between 25–35 francs; some theaters sell discounted daytime tickets and tickets for Wednesday shows as well, and Parisians always look forward to the annual *18F à 18h*, or 18-franc tickets at 6pm or afterwards, a weeklong, citywide film festival in the second week of February.

Essential to making your choice are weekly publications like *L'Officiel de Spectacle* or, better, *Pariscope;* both have complete film listings and are available at all newsstands. If you speak French, you can also ring **Allô Ciné** (tel 40 30 20 10), a free, 24-hour film line that dispenses information on current shows according to neighborhood. Paris has recently seen both an impressive renovation of movie theaters and the construction of state-of-the-art cineplexes like the **Gaumont Grand Ecran Italie** at the Place d'Italie in the 13th arrondissement, which boasts Europe's largest movie screen.

If any single neighborhood in Paris is especially rich in art-house cinemas, it's the Left Bank, which has a gloriously dense concentration of tiny but always comfortable little theaters where you can catch not only a rerun of *Klute* or *The Girl Can't Help It*, but treats like the latest locally made box-office smash from Guatemala. The best-known of these is the showcase theater of a small chain of old-style, student-proletariat, revival houses which continue to survive the video revolution: **Action Rive Gauche** near the Sorbonne. Otherwise, the Champs-Elysées, boulevard du Montparnasse, and what are known as Les Grands Boulevards (the Haussmann-built boulevards—boulevard des Italiens, boulevard Montmartre, and boulevard Poissonière) all running east from the Opera, are the main, first-run districts. The multiplexes in the ghastly subterranean shopping mall at Les Halles are popular, too. **La Pagode**, which has two screens and occupies a pagoda that was shipped piecemeal from Japan at the turn of the century, is surely the most charming cinema in Paris and is worth going out of your way for. **Le Grand Rex**, on the boulevard Poissonière, is a stunning art-deco picture palace that seats 2,600. Serious film buffs should also check out **Le Cinémathèque Française**, which specializes in funky retrospectives; the **Vidéothèque de Paris**, a fabulous film archive where for 30 francs you can install yourself at a video console and call up images of Paris from every film that's ever been made; and the way-cool **L'Entrepôt**, where an arty crowd relishes three screens usually showing Third World or new-director films in a converted warehouse.

The Index

Action Rive Gauche. The flagship of a small, first-rate chain of Left Bank revival houses that was founded in 1967 and made its reputation producing fresh prints of out-of-circulation films. Their forte is thirties, forties, and fifties Hollywood, although they occasionally feature French directors and have recently been offering hilarious programs of French films from the seventies.... *Tel 43 29 44 40 (recorded information); 5, rue des Ecoles, 75005; Métro Cardinal-Lemoine.*

Auditorium du Châtelet. The twice-monthly jazz concerts here have become very popular, but the auditorium also hosts a wide range of other music events, including various ethnic music festivals. Parisians appreciate its central location in Les Halles.... *Tel 42 36 13 90; Forum des Halles, Porte Saint Eustache, 75001; Métro Les Halles.*

La Bataclan. Though it's recently hosted some of the hottest dance nights in town on the weekend, the Bataclan remains a concert venue par excellence. Lots of atmosphere, good acoustics, and generally outstanding programming make this a superb place to take in tunes.... *Tel 47 00 55 22; 50, bd. Voltaire, 75011; Métro Oberkampf.*

Les Blancs-Manteaux. As is true of most café-théâtres these days, the bill of fare at the venerable Blancs-Manteaux is tamer than it was during the glory days of the sixties. Instead of social protest, à la anti-Vietnam, these twin theaters often feature satirical dramas designed to lampoon the polite, professional, thirtysomething couples who make up most of the audience.... *Tel 48 87 15 84; 15, rue des Blancs-Manteaux, 75004; Métro Rambuteau.*

Les Bouffes du Nord. With its crumbling walls and dirt floor, Les Bouffes, as it's affectionately known, is one of the most magical theater houses in Paris. It's home base for British director Peter Brook and his polyglot international troupe of actors, who do everything from Shakespeare, Christopher Marlowe, and ancient Greek dramas to avant-garde improvisations. Productions here are almost unfailingly good, and it's a fantastic experience to see a play in these surroundings.... *Tel 46 07 34 50; 37 bis, bd. de la Chapelle, 75010; Métro La Chapelle.*

Café de la Gare. Long before he charmed malls full of Americans in *Green Card,* Gérard Depardieu was just another fledgling thespian at this lively, often bawdy theater in a converted stable in the Marais. The theater still does very funny one-man or one-woman shows, but you'll need some knowledge of French politics, showbiz personalities, and Parisian gossip to catch the hot-potato punchlines.... *Tel 42 78 52 51; 41, rue du Temple, 75004; Métro Hôtel-de-Ville.*

Cartoucherie de Vincennes. A fine example of what a proper national arts budget can accomplish, this complex of five theaters in the Bois de Vincennes on the eastern edge of the city opened in 1970 and has since produced some of the most innovative theater in Paris. Ariane Mnouchkine, one of the most accomplished avant-garde directors in Europe, still directs at the Théâtre du Soleil, one of the five here, and productions are known for their dramatic staging and provocative content. Ticket prices vary, but are often much gentler than those found elsewhere.... *Tel 47 00 15 87; route de Champs-de-Manoeuvre, Bois de Vincennes, 75012; Métro Château de Vincennes and then shuttle bus Cartoucherie or bus 112.*

Cathédrale de Notre-Dame. Begun in 1163 by Bishop Maurice de Sully, this glorious, Gothic cathedral (the most famous church in Paris) was not completed until 1345. The regular Sunday evening organ concerts here are a splendid opportunity to gape at the three rose windows while listening to some wonderful music. The church also holds other concerts on a regular basis.... *Tel 42 34 56 10; pl. du Parvis-Notre-Dame, Ile de la Cité, 75004; Métro Cité.*

Châtelet–Théâtre Musical de Paris. Under the direction of Stephane Lissner, the Châtelet has become Paris's third major opera house, with programming often more star-filled than Opéra Bastille's. A preferred venue for new productions, such as a recent *Don Carlos* with José Van Dam and rising star tenor Roberto Alagna. The theater also hosts visiting companies, such as Berlin's Deutschoper.... *Tel 40 28 28 40; 1, pl. du Châtelet, 7500; Métro Châtelet.*

La Cigale. A relatively decent concert hall, but avoid the balcony. Originally a vaudeville house, it still has a slightly frosty, music hall feel with its somber black and gray decor.... *Tel 49 25 81 75; 120, bd. Rochechouart, 75018; Métro Pigalle.*

La Cinémathèque Française. The granddaddy of quality film theaters all over the world. The brainchild of film freaks Georges Franju and Henri Langlois, it opened in 1936, and today is the most respected serious film venue in the world. It shows a regular program of themed retrospectives and also holds conferences and offers classes.... *Tel 47 04 24 24; Palais de Chaillot, 7, rue Albert-de-Mun, 75116; Métro Trocadéro.*

La Cité de la Musique. On the edge of the city, where the municipal slaughterhouses used to be, this impressive new complex offers a great range of programming and also has a very slick and popular postmodern cafe that serves light meals. The oval-shaped concert hall is as yet too young to have acquired any particular aural reputation, but was designed to be friendly to all kinds of music. Note that you can attend rehearsals for free if you reserve up to three weeks in advance.... *Tel 44 84 45 45 (tickets), 44 84 44 84 (information); 221, av. Jean-Jaures, 75019; Métro Porte de Pantin.*

Comédie Française–Salle Richelieu. All of the glory of classic French theater is found in this hallowed theater, one of the most charming in Paris. If you torturously read your way through *Le Bourgeois Gentilhomme* in a French civilization class many moons ago, this might be your chance to give French drama its real due. They also occasionally produce serious but lesser known 19th- and 20th-century plays.... *Tel 40 15 00 15; 2, rue Richelieu, 75002; Métro Palais-Royal.*

Comédie Française–Théâtre du Vieux Colombier. This handsomely renovated old theater became the Left Bank annex of the Comédie Française in 1993, and does a generally tempting program of serious well-acted and directed plays.... *Tel 44 39 87 00; 21, rue du Vieux-Colombier, 75004; Métro Saint-Sulpice.*

Eglise Sainte-Chapelle. There are few corners of Paris more magnificent than this Gothic chapel built by Louis IX in 1298 to house the Crown of Thorns and other precious relics. One of the most remarkable concert venues in Paris, so tickets sell out quickly, regardless of what's on.... *Tel 43 54 30 09; 4, bd. du Palais, Ile de la Cité, 75001; Métro Cité.*

Eglise Saint-Eustache. For centuries this was the church of Les Halles, the main food market of Paris, which was formerly across the street before being transferred to the suburbs. Its 8,000-pipe organ makes it a choice venue for concerts; musicians love its acoustics. Free organ concerts are held daily from 5–5:30pm, while other concerts require tickets.... *Tel 40 26 47 99; rue du Jour, 75001; Métro Les Halles.*

Eglise Saint-Germain-des-Prés. The Romanesque bell tower of this church, a symbol of the Saint Germain neighborhood, gives a charming rustic feel to the surrounding area. The first church on this site was built in the sixth century and was followed by a Benedictine abbey that was one of the most powerful in medieval France; only traces of it remain today. During the organ and occasional choral concerts given here, inspect the murals painted by Hippolyte Flandrin during the mid-19th century.... *Tel 43 25 41 71; 3, pl. du Saint-Germain-des-Prés, 75006; Métro Saint-Germain-des-Prés.*

Eglise Saint-Julien-le-Pauvre. One of the oldest and most atmospheric churches in Paris, this one was built in the 12th century as a way station for pilgrims. Today, it's mostly ruined, but the Romanesque chapel, home of a Greek Orthodox congregation, is a popular and powerful venue for classical concerts.... *Tel 43 54 52 16; 1, rue Saint-Julien-le-Pauvre, 75005; Métro St-Michel.*

Eglise Saint-Louis-en-L'Ile. Curiously, in view of its location, the Ile Saint-Louis is one of the least spoiled districts of Paris, and remains one of its chicest residential neighborhoods and a choice place to stroll in the evening. This *mis en scène* enhances the pleasure you'll find by attending a classical concert at this charming baroque church.... *Tel 46 34 11 60; 21, rue Saint-Louis-en-L'Ile, 75004; Métro Pont-Marie.*

Elysée Montmartre. This funky, old music hall with wooden floors and a moody dose of art-nouveau charm is a wonderful place to see a concert. The bill varies, but runs from rap to visiting choral groups from Brittany.... *Tel 42 55 81 47; 72, bd. Rochechouart, 75018; Métro Anvers.*

L'Entrepôt. Feeling a bit metaphysical and ready to inter yourself in darkness to brood? This is the place, and one of the few in Paris today where you'll run into other people who care passionately about what happens on the screen. In addition to excellent films, the theater also has a good film-oriented book shop, a bar, and a café where you can do a Jean Seberg or Zazie number as you see fit.... *Tel 45 43 41 63; 7–9, rue Francis-de-Pressensé, 75001; Métro Pernéty.*

Espace Kiron. A small, simple venue that often hosts one of the many contemporary dance companies working in Paris.... *Tel 44 65 11 50; 10, rue de la Vacquerie, 75011; Métro Voltaire.*

FNAC. Every branch in this chain of book-music stores also has a ticket counter where you can nail tickets for almost anything that's going on in Paris and pay by credit card. Inconveniently, you have to come by in person to obtain your tickets because the stores don't sell by phone.... *Tel 40 41 40 00; Forum des Halles, 1/5, rue Pierre Lescot, level three, 75001; Métro Les Halles. Closed Sun.*

Gaumont Grand Ecran Italie. Though this triplex includes Paris's state-of-the-art, big-screen cinema, the two accompanying screens are oddly cramped and ordinary. What attracts sometimes rowdy crowds on the weekends is the laser show that precedes the feature in the big-screen room, and even if you're not a testosterone-plagued teenager,

PARIS ⏝ THE ARTS

you'll probably still think it's pretty cool.... *Tel 45 80 77 00; 30, pl. d'Italie, 75013; Métro Place d'Italie.*

Le Grand Rex. The films shown at this exultantly art-deco theater vary, but for real film lovers the experience of sharing the big screen with 2,600 viewers is pretty spectacular in and of itself.... *Tel 42 36 83 93; 1, bd. Poisonnière, 75002; Métro Bonne Nouvelle.*

Kiosque Théâtre. The two branches of this discount-ticket outlet usually have a good offer of same-day theater tickets. No telephone sales.... *15, pl. de la Madeleine, 75009; Métro Madeleine. Square in front of the Gare Montparnasse, 75014; Métro Montparnasse-Bienvenue. Closed Sun and Mon.*

Le Lapin Agile. A cabaret made famous early in the century by artistic habitues such as Picasso, this atmospheric club in Montmartre keeps on the cabaret tradition with poetry readings and comic sketches. Come prepared with a good French vocabulary in order to pick up the subtleties of what's happening on stage.... *Tel 46 06 85 75 22, rue des Saules, 75018; Métro Lamarch-Caulaincourt. Cosed Mon. 100 F cover, 80F for students with ID cards.*

La Madeleine. Looking rather smarter since its pediment and facade were cleaned in 1995, this somewhat gloomy, neoclassical church does, however, offer a pleasant location for the concerts, often choral, that are held here.... *Tel 44 51 69 00; pl. de la Madeleine, 75008; Métro Madeleine.*

Maison de Radio France. The home of Radio France, much respected for the excellent quality of its classical-music programming and its musical programs in general, is a vast, round, characterless building that can be difficult to find your way into. It's worth the effort, though, because their admirably varied offering is not only excellent but often free. This is home base for both the Orchestre National de Paris and the Orchestre Philharmonique de Radio France. If you're really keen, you can write to them in advance of your visit and request a program guide.... *Tel 42 30 15 16; 116, av. du President Kennedy, 75016; Métro Ranelagh or Passy.*

Musée de Cluny. Renowned for its *Lady and the Unicorn* tapestries and other intriguing medieval artifacts, this museum sponsors one of the most appealing regularly scheduled weekend concert series in Paris, often featuring medieval or Renaissance music and very reasonably priced.... *Tel 43 25 61 91; 6, pl. Paul-Painlevé, 75005; Métro Cluny-La Sorbonne.*

Musée du Louvre. Many consider this to be the world's greatest museum, but the classical music concerts are a draw, too.... *Tel 40 20 50 50/general information, 40 20 51 51/recorded information; Cour Napoleon, 75001; Métro Palais Royale—Musée du Louvre. Closed Tues. Aile Richelieu open Mon until 9:45pm, entire museum open Wed until 9:45pm.*

Musée Nationale d'Histoire Naturelle. If you're traveling with kids, they'll surely go for the dinosaur skeletons exhibited at this pleasant and well-organized museum of natural history in the Jardins des Plantes. The museum also shows children-oriented nature films.... *Tel 40 79 30 00; 57, rue Cuvier, Jardins des Plantes, 75005; Métro Jussieu or Gare d'Austerlitz. Open Thur until 10pm.*

Musée d'Orsay. Once an unused train station, this is where to find the Impressionists' works, as well as a superb collection of work by the Romantics, Realists, Surrealists, and Pointillists.... *Tel 40 49 48 14; 1, rue de Bellechasse, 75007; Métro Solferino. Closed Mon. Open Thur until 9:45pm.*

Odéon–Théâtre de L'Europe. An essential venue for serious theatergoers, because the two theaters here—the main house and the intimate 80-seat Petit Odéon—offer a regular program of quality European drama of varying vintages. Most productions are generally done both in French and in the original language, which means that you might chance upon a visiting production from Dublin's Abbey Theater or the breaking works of a young Portuguese or Danish playwright. Everything about this theater—the building, the administration, the programming, the casting, and the directing—bespeaks the very best of European culture. Do not, by the way, be tempted to dine at La Mediterranée, the restaurant in front of the theater; Jean Cocteau may have designed a lot of the furnishings, but the food's dreadful,

PARIS ⟨ **THE ARTS**

and it's become almost exclusively the preserve of badly informed Japanese travelers.... *Tel 44 41 36 36; 1, pl. de l'Odéon, 75006; Métro Odéon.*

Olympia. An all-purpose concert venue for mostly mainstream, middle-class events, this place at least has the advantage of a central location. It's also worth following for anyone who loves traditional French music along the lines of Mireille Mathieu.... *Tel 47 42 82 45; 28, bd. des Capucines, 75009; Métro Madeleine.*

Opéra Comique–Salle Favart. A charming, small opera house, originally founded in 1782 by the Duke of Choiseul, which today shows light operas with smaller casts and operettas by Offenbach and Johann Strauss.... *Tel 41 44 45 46; 5, rue Favart, 75002; Métro Richelieu-Drouout.*

Opéra de Paris–Bastille. Beached whale, misplaced ocean liner, or public toilet? Uruguayan architect Carlos Ott's massive monument with its 2,700-seat auditorium opened in 1991 with the intention of offering opera at reasonable prices. Seats now cost just as much as they do at the Palais Garnier, but there the theater alone is worth the price of admission. Acoustics are not what they should be either, but with state-of-the-art technical facilities and revolving stages, it is the place to see extravagant, large-cast-and-chorus operas such as Berlioz's *Les Troyens* or Verdi's *Aida*..... *Tel 44 73 13 00; pl. de la Bastille, 75011; Métro Bastille.*

Opéra de Paris–Palais Garnier. The world's ultimate opera house since it was built by architect Charles Garnier in 1875. It's a sumptuous Second Empire monument with a swirling marble staircase and a six-ton crystal chandelier. The Opéra Bastille opened in 1991; the Garnier's been the home of the Paris Opera Ballet, but smaller operas such as Mozart's *Così fan tutte* are still performed here. The place for opera in Paris.... *Tel 40 01 17 89 (recorded information), 43 43 96 96 (phone reservations), 44 73 13 00 (general information); pl. de l'Opéra, 75009, Métro Opéra.*

La Pagode. This intriguing movie house is tucked away in a quiet and intensely bourgeois corner of the seventh arrondissement. This pagoda was assembled in 1896 by

Artistide Boucicault, founder of the Bon Marché department store, as a gift for his wife (who had a penchant for things Asian). The tearoom is a very pleasant place to take a time out before or after showtime. The main auditorium has a remarkable Franco-Japanese decor.... *Tel 40 30 20 10; 57, rue de Babylone, 75007; Métro Saint-François Xavier.*

Palais des Congress. Though most Parisians dislike this big, modern auditorium in the ugly seventies-vintage office complex at the Porte Maillot, the large space has good acoustics and sight lines. It's often used for concerts, dance performances, and solo shows.... *Tel 40 68 00 05; Porte Maillot, 75016; Métro Porte Maillot.*

Palais Omnisports de Paris-Bercy. Representing a pretentious nadir of French seventies architecture, this stadium devours almost everyone who performs here; it's too big and completely charmless. It's also in a rather inconvenient location. It's worth braving if there's something going on that you just can't miss, but if you're in the mood to rock to whoever's around, try one of the other venues.... *Tel 43 46 12 21; 8, bd. de Bercy, 75012; Métro Bercy.*

Paris User's Guide Information Line. An English-speaking help-line that arranges opera tickets and provides general arts information about performances.... *Tel 44 29 12 20.*

Peniche Opéra. The unlikely setting—a barge in the canal Saint Martin—adds to the fun of a generally appealing program that runs to mini-operas, operatic concerts, and solo recitals.... *Tel 43 49 08 15; 200, quai de Jemmapes, 75010; Métro Jaures.*

Poche Montparnasse. This small theater with two performing spaces is almost all that's left of the theater district that once flourished around the Gare Montparnasse. The Poche Montparnasse favors intelligent, well-acted productions of serious French dramatists like Marivaux. It's generally worth risking an unknown play or author here because the work staged is so reliably good. If you're coming by Métro and are unfamiliar with the Montparnasse station, don't cut it too close to curtain time—this labyrinth was designed by a sadist of the first order.... *Tel 45 48 92 97; 75, bd. du Montparnasse, 75014; Métro Montparnasse-Bienvenüe.*

Salle Gaveau. This charming, old-fashioned hall is one of the best venues in Paris for piano recitals, usually running to Liszt, Debussy, Fauré, and Chopin. Performers range from well-known stars such as Pollini to promising younger players in town from cities like London, Prague, and San Francisco.... *Tel 49 53 05 07; 45, rue de la Boétie, 75008; Métro Miromesnil.*

Salle Pleyel. This rather austere but acoustically correct hall is the home of the Orchestre de Paris, which means it's a regular venue for big-name international soloists and conductors. Parisians are loyal to their orchestra, and turn out in well-dressed droves when any important soloist comes to perform with it.... *Tel 45 61 53 00; 252, rue du Faubourg St-Honoré, 75008; Métro Ternes.*

Théâtre des Champs-Elysées. A well-dressed, older crowd frequents this attractive theater on one of the most expensive shopping streets in the world. The programming's eclectic—Pierre Boulez directing the Vienna Philharmonic one week, the Kirov Ballet the next, and then maybe an opera or a lyric recital.... *Tel 49 52 50 50; 15, av. Montaigne, 75008; Métro Alma-Marceau.*

Théâtre National de Chaillot. This gorgeous theater, part of the complex built for the Universal Exhibition of 1937, is home to director Jérôme Savary, who favors lavishly produced, floppy extravaganzas that often have a humor quotient just above the banana-peel level.... *Tel 47 27 81 15; 1, place du Trocadéro, 75016; Métro Trocadéro.*

Théâtre Nesle. This minuscule theater is the leading stage for English-language productions in Paris, and generally features performances by one of the city's two or three English-language theater companies. The best among them include Dear Conjunction, Compagnie Robert Cordier, On Stage Theater Company, and Gare St-Lazare Company. The offer tends to run to serious drama by the likes of Harold Pinter and Bertolt Brecht.... *Tel 46 34 61 04; 8, rue de Nesle, 75006; Métro Odéon.*

Théâtre de la Ville. This contemporary theater is the primary venue for contemporary dance in Paris and is well-regarded for its innovative programming. If you're a real devotee of modern dance, call as soon as you arrive to see what's on; you'll likely find a performer or a company you've never seen before. Regulars include the intriguing Flemish bad-boy of Belgian dance, Jan Fabry. Belgian Anne Teresa de Keersmaeker, the Ballets Culberg from Sweden, American Carolyn Carlson, the first-rate Japanese Sankai Juku, and Pina Bausch.... *Tel 42 74 22 77; 2, place du Châtelet, 75004; Métro Châtelet.*

Vidéothèque de Paris. This fantastic film archive is proof that Paris is the most vain city in the world—absolutely every appearance that the city's ever made in film is available here. More than 5,000 films in the film library and two screens.... *Tel 40 26 34 30; 2, Grand Galerie, Forum des Halles–Porte Saint Eustache, 75001; Métro Les Halles.*

Virgin Megastore. This British audio chain also has a ticket counter and stays open late.... *Tel 44 68 44 08; 52, av. des Champs-Elysées, 75008; Métro Franklin-D.-Roosevelt.*

PARIS ◡ THE ARTS

spo

rts

Although the preferred
workout of most Parisians
centers on the small-
muscle movements
required to deftly wield a
knife and fork, the city is
well equipped with sports

facilities. The difference is that Parisians have never developed the compulsive attitude toward exercise that prevails in North America. Interest in spectator sports in Paris generally follows rather predictable sociological lines. Tennis (like the famous **Tournée Roland Garros,** as the French Open is called) is the preferred sport of the city's haute bourgeoisie, which also occasionally attends the odd horse-racing event. Many young professionals like rugby, while *le football,* as the national sport, soccer, is called, is considered *très populaire* in the same way that baseball is the United States. The recent bribery scandals surrounding media tycoon Bernard Tapie, owner of the football club in the city of Valenciennes, have tarnished the sport in the eyes of numerous Parisians, and many cool young city-dwellers are much more interested in basketball than soccer. Touring U.S. basketball teams regularly sell out at the Omnisports de Bercy, partly a reflection of the fascination that well-bred, young Parisians have for American inner-city, hip-hop culture. Depending upon what interests you, call **Allô Sports** (tel 42 76 54 54), a free, English-speaking phone line that offers information on sports and sporting events in Paris and its environs.

The Lowdown

Where they play... The main venues for spectator sports are the **Parc de Princes** (tel 49 87 29 29; 24, rue du Commandant Guilbaud, 75016; Métro Porte d'Auteuil), where the city's winning soccer team, Paris Saint-Germain, plays, and **Palais Omnisports de Paris—Bercy** (tel 43 46 12 21; 8, bd. de Bercy, 75012; Métro Bercy), which embodies a pretentious nadir of French seventies architecture. On the menu are events ranging from indoor tennis tournaments to windsurfing competitions.

Soccer... **Parc des Princes** is the home of **Paris Saint-Germain,** the city's soccer team. The Parc will be replaced by a lavish new stadium, which is scheduled to open in 1998, in time for the World Cup games. If you're a soccer fan, this team is on the rise and has recently won a variety of important European matches; their season runs from late July through early May (tel 49 87 29 29; 24, rue du Commandant-Guilbaud, 75016; Métro Porte d'Auteuil).

Bowling... If you're feeling desperate to knock down some pins, the **Bowling-Mouffetard** (tel 43 31 09 35; 13, rue Gracieuse, 75005; Métro Monge; open daily until 2am; 20F) is the best bowling alley within the city proper and attracts an interesting, often bibulous, crowd. Deep in the heart of the Latin Quarter, this eight-lane bowling alley is a great night out if you're seeking an antidote to heavy cultural feeding during the day. Its low prices draw a friendly, young crowd. A bit off the beaten track, in the Jardin d'Acclimation, a leisure center in the middle of the Bois de Boulogne, **Bowling de Paris** (tel 40 67 94 00; Jardin d'Acclimation, Bois de Boulogne, 75016; Métro Porte Maillot; open daily until 2am; 20F per game, 10F for shoe rental) boasts 24 lanes and is the best bowling alley in Paris. This spot is popular with professional bowlers and couples on dates.

Health clubs... You can buy a day-pass to work out at health clubs with late-opening hours like the **Club Quartier Latin** and **Espace Vit'Halles.** At these two clubs you'll find people pumping away just like back home, but most Parisians do sports for pleasure rather than physical punishment. **Club Quartier Latin** (tel 43 54 82 45; 19, rue de Pontoise, 75005; Métro Maubert-Mutualité; open Monday through Friday until midnight, until 7:30pm on weekends; 60F day pass) has good facilities and convenient hours. This club is particularly popular with English-speaking locals. There are squash courts, calisthenic classes, and a day pass that also includes admission to the adjacent Piscine de Pontoise, one of the most attractive indoor pools in Paris. At **Espace Vit'Halles** (a name that shows the French are no more immune to cloying puns than anyone else) you'll find lots of models frequenting this gym, which is popular among the serious workout crowd in Paris. Among Paris clubs, this one comes closest to a standard-issue American gym, with several circuits of machines, free weights, and aerobics classes (tel 42 77 21 71; place Beaubourg, 48, rue Rambuteau, 75004; Métro Rambuteau; open until 10pm Monday through Friday; 80F day pass).

Skating... Are you skating with or without ice? The **Patinoire de Boulogne** (tel 46 21 00 96; 1, rue Victor Griffuelhes, Boulogne; Métro Marcel Sembat; open Tuesday through Friday until 11:30pm, Saturday until midnight; 30F admission, 20F skate rental), an enormous ice rink where French Olympic champion Surya Bonaly works out, is open late most nights. French skaters are decorous, and this is an appealingly polite place with good facilities, including skate rental. **La Main Jaune** is both a roller disco and a roller rink; both attract a very frisky, young crowd. Though it's most popular as a roller-disco venue, you can also come here just to skate. A curious mixture of rich teenagers from central Paris blends with hip-hop kids from the housing projects on the other side of the *peripherique*, or beltway, that encircles Paris (tel 47 63 26 47; place de la Porte Champerret, 75017; Métro Porte de Champerret; open Friday, Saturday, and the nights before public holidays; 70F cover, 15F skate rental).

Pool... To take aim at some balls, the city has several first-rate pool halls. **Hôtel Concorde Saint-Lazare** (tel 40 08 44 44; Hôtel Concorde Saint-Lazare, 108, rue Saint-Lazare, 75008; Métro Saint-Lazare; open daily until 2am; average rate 60F/hour) is the best-dressed pool hall in Paris, with cigar-smoking captains of industry and young stockbroker types wielding their cues as long-suffering dates look on. Their consolation is that this turn-of-the-century salon is lushly attractive and was decorated by fashion designer Sonia Rykiel. The friendly, low-key atmosphere of **Blue-Billiard** (tel 43 55 87 21; 11, rue Saint-Maur, 75010; open daily until 2am; 50F/hour) near the place de la République, makes it a good place to shoot a game or two before some serious night-crawling in the nearby Bastille. **Académie de Billard Clichy-Montmartre** (tel 48 78 32 85; 84, rue de Clichy, 75009; Métro Place de Clichy; open Monday through Thursday and Sunday until 3am, Friday and Saturday until 5:30am; rates average 55F/hour) is a busy and agreeably louche pool hall with a diverse crowd of regulars. It's always busy at night, when this vast, high-ceilinged room becomes thick with smoke and people winking at each other in the gaudy, gilt mirrors.

Swimming... Paris has a fine choice of generally immaculate public swimming pools. The **Piscine de Pontoise** (tel 43 53 82 45; 19, rue de Pontoise, 75005; Métro Maubert-Mutualité; open Monday through Thursday until midnight; 40F admission) is a fantastic art-deco pool that's connected to the Club Quartier Latin. Centrally located, this pool has much charm, including a vintage skylight. It also attracts an interesting crowd of friendly, solitary swimmers. You might stick a toe in at the **Piscine Suzanne-Berlioux,** (tel 42 36 98 44; 10, place de la Rotonde, 75001; Métro Les Halles; open until 10pm Tuesday through Friday) an Olympic-size pool. If there were a soundtrack for the action at this skylit modern facility in the center of town, it would definitely be by Barry White. Come here to do your laps and to make new friends. If you're of a botanical bent, or looking for a quiet place to chat, an adjacent greenhouse is filled with tropical plants. The young clientele pays a lot of attention to hair and makeup. Surely the most unusual place to take a dip is **Aquaboulevard** (tel 40 60 10 00; 4, rue Louis-Armand, 75015; Métro Balard; open Monday through Thursday and Sunday until 11pm, Friday and Saturday until midnight; 65F adult admission, 50F children), an enormous leisure complex on the southern edge of town that has a vast indoor-outdoor pool, slides, a wave pool, and a variety of other facilities including tennis courts, a gym, and a putting green. This place was conceived for family fun and is popular with folks who can't get to Martinique during the winter or Brittany during the summer, but also draws a singles crowd after work. It's clean, well organized, and your unique opportunity to paddle around in an indoor tropical lagoon while in Paris. Though there's something rather antic about this place, the facilities are excellent, and it can be unexpected fun. During the summer at night, a younger crowd of singles gathers here to sip drinks with little paper parasols and show off gym-toned bodies.

Tennis... If you go nowhere without your tennis racket, the best place in Paris, where public courts are often very crowded, is the **Centre Sportif La Faluère** (tel 43 74 40 93; route de la Pyramide, Bois de Vincennes, 75012; Métro Château de Vincennes; open Monday through Saturday until 10pm, Sunday until 8pm) in the Bois de Vincennes. Here you'll find 21 courts, but be forewarned that many are reserved by various tennis clubs, and that they're especially busy during after-work hours.

By bicycle... **Paris Vélo** offers Paris-by-Night bicycle tours of the city, with bilingual guides. The itinerary varies, but they're designed to avoid the most heavily trafficked neighborhoods, and include stops for drinks and photos. You don't have to be a fitness freak either, because Paris is a relatively flat city. (tel 43 37 59 22; 2, rue du Fer-à-Moulin, 75005; Métro Censier-Daubenton. 150F includes bike rental).

By boat... A nighttime trip on a **Bateaux-Mouche** is great experience, too. The Seine, though narrow and aqueous, still functions as the greatest boulevard in Paris. Lining its meticulously tended banks are most of the capital's greatest monuments, and until afloat you never completely understand that for centuries the river has been the centerpiece around which the rest of the city has been very knowingly laid out. For something truly kitsch, the **Bateaux Mouches dinner cruise** leaves the Pont de l'Alma every summer evening at 8:30, so book a table on the top deck and decide which music you prefer—they offer classical and dance (semi-pop) tracks. Don't come expecting one of the greatest gourmet moments in your life, but the food's just fine, even a little better than you might expect, and it's interesting to see how the French manage even large-scale feeding with a certain finesse. The service is very good, though—the friendly, multilingual waiters communicate their orders to the kitchen with computerized walkie-talkies—and you can have all the champagne or wine you like, which you should bear in mind vis-à-vis the price of this expedition. It's expensive, but then consider that the tariff includes all drinks, dinner, and entertainment, and it seems almost a good value. (tel 42 25 96 10; Pont de l'Alma, 75008; Métro Alma-Marceau. Dinner cruise daily at 8:30pm, 500F; regular cruises every half hour until 11pm, 40F). Easier to get to and somewhat more intimate, **Les Vedettes du Pont Neuf** (tel 46 33 98 38; 1, square du Vert-Galant, 75001; Métro Pont-Neuf; departures daily from 9–10:30pm, 3F) are smaller boats that leave every half-hour from a launch on the western tip of the Ile de la Cité. The canned, bilingual English-French commentary is hokey, so consider bringing a Walkman if you don't want to hear inanities such as *"Voilà le Pont Marie!"* (here is Mary's Bridge).

Car racing... The only place to see the Le Mans car race is on TV, but if trolling through the city's museums has brought on an urgent need to burn some rubber, head for this racing center. Strapped into a minicar, you can zoom around the track at speeds reaching 300 kilometers an hour. The crowd at **The Racing Center** is a mix of teens and machos (tel 47 27 56 56; 67, av. Raymond Poincaré, 75016; Métro Victor-Hugo; open until 11:30pm).

PARIS SPORTS

hangi

ng out

One of the most alluring
terms in the French
language is *se flaner*, which
roughly translated means
to lounge aimlessly. The
French verb, however, does
not carry the same hidden

value judgment as the comparable English expression; you don't find articles in French magazines telling you 100 things you can do while standing in line at the supermarket. The French, thank God, still value leisure as an absolute good in and of itself, and there's no better city in Europe in which to master this art than Paris, especially at night. Unlike New York, for example, where the night is nearly as busy as the day and you can get a haircut, have your shoes repaired, down a bowl of linguine with clam sauce, or go to the gym at 3am, after-dark Paris becomes secretive, intimate, and mostly empty. Stroll the arcades of the **Palais Royal** or sit in the **Place des Vosges** listening to the fountain splatter, and you'll sense that, by night, Paris is teasing and flirtatious, with a delicate and delicious atmosphere of sensual expectation.

The Lowdown

Where to walk... Teeming during the day with tourists from every corner of the planet, after midnight huge parts of the city are nearly deserted, which means that this is your chance to savor the sights without the distraction of thousands of logo-printed T-shirts surrounding you. So, depending upon who you are, put on your spike heels, your penny loafers, or your jogging shoes, and walk. The **Place des Vosges**, in the Marais; the **Place de la Concorde**, next to the Tuileries Gardens; and the **Palais Royal**, across the street from the Louvre, are excellent destinations for a nocturnal amble. Follow the banks of the Seine; walk from the **Place de la Bastille** to the **Place de la Concorde**; take in the whole length of the **boulevard Saint Germain**; explore the **Champs de Mars**, the park and gardens around the Eiffel Tower, if you're in search of beauty and solitude. If you prefer people-watching and the buzz of a crowd, head for one of the city's pulse points. You can sit on the steps of the **Opéra Bastille**, in the place de la Bastille; hang around in front of the **Centre Pompidou**; tarry by the fountains of the **Place des Innocents** in Les Halles; or on the Left Bank at the **Place Saint Michel**. For the closest Parisian approximation of Times Square or Piccadilly Circus, try the **Place de Clichy**, or the more diminutive **Place Pigalle**; both offer relatively tame tastes of honky-tonk to tour-bus tourists, as well as being vital arty zones for locals. **Les Halles** also remains busy well into the night, especially along the rue Saint Denis, the rue des Lombards, and the rue de la Ferronerie. You might also troll up or down the Champs-Elysées, but don't do so in the hopes of seeing Parisian elegance—though its been handsomely remodeled, this famous avenue is filling up with fast-food places from one end to the other, and the crowd is mostly suburban teenagers in jogging suits.

Walking on the wild side... For an entirely different sort of nighttime wander, head for the **rue Saint-Denis**, which starts at Châtelet in the heart of town and runs north, or try the **boulevard de Clichy** near Montmartre. What you'll find along these two streets are peep shows, porno parlors, strip and live-sex shows, and a rather woebegone offering of independent contractors lurking in doorways. The rue Saint-Denis is mostly frequented by harmless and horny teenagers, while the boulevard de Clichy lives off of a middle-aged, tour-bus crowd from places like Birmingham, Frankfurt, Basel, and Liège. Needless to say, beware the barkers and the watered-down and exorbitantly priced drinks pressed on you by the hostesses.

Best window-shopping... To enjoy this activity, best done by night, window-shoppers can choose from two great strolls: along the **avenue Montaigne**, with luxury boutiques from Chanel to the flagship boutique of Christian Dior, and the **rue Saint-Honoré**, starting at the corner of the rue Jean Mermoz and heading all the way east to the rue Castiglione. The French term for window-shopping translates literally as "window-licking"; a walk along these two stretches may explain why. The rectangle defined by the **rue du Bac**, the **rue de l'Université**, **the Seine**, and the **rue de Seine**, is another fantastic place to window-shop at night because it's densely packed with art galleries and antiques shops, many of which are handsomely lit and imaginatively decorated.

Bird's-eye views... Some of the best views of Paris cost nothing. You get fine panoramas from the steps of **Sacré Coeur** in Montmartre (35, rue Chevalier-de-la-Barre, 75018; Métro Abbesses) and the top floor of the **Centre Pompidou** museum (rue Beaubourg, 75004; Métro Châtelet-Les Halles), but after the disaster of the **Tour Maine-Montparnasse** (33, av. de Maine, 75014; Métro Montparnasse; open daily until 10pm, 42F admission) in the seventies, the city planners wisely prohibited any further skyscrapers within the heart of the city. If you climb to the top of this 42-story, circa-1974 blight on the local landscape, you'll see clusters of towers beyond the Arc de Triomphe in the sterile new business neighborhood known as La Défense, and also to the south around the edges of the 13th arrondissement. Otherwise, Paris remains a gorgeous 19th-century city, webbed with boulevards by Baron Haussmann, who radically redeveloped the city between 1853 and 1870. The ultimate view of Paris, however, is from the **Eiffel Tower**, which is itself magnificent at night. Here you can either pay admission for a ride to the top or, if you're well-dressed and feeling feisty, try to gain access to the elegant and very expensive Jules Verne restaurant and have a drink at the bar. There's no set policy on whether this is a sure thing—the restaurant generally discourages people from coming for drinks—but if you look the part, it usually works. (Eiffel Tower: tel 44 11 23 45; Champ de Mars, 75007; Métro Bir-Hakeim; open daily until 11pm. Admission: 20F, first floor; 38F, second floor; 55F, third floor.)

City bridges... The vainest city of all never ceases to embellish itself, and its latest project is the illumination of all 33 of the bridges that span the Seine within the city limits. The best way to appreciate the subtlety of this lighting is to bring a bottle of chilled champagne with you (call **Allô Champagne** for 24-hour delivery service; tel 44 53 93 33) and settle into one of the rounded niches that are built into the **Pont Neuf**, not only the most beautiful bridge in Paris, but a superb place from which to stare at the city. To the east, you'll see La Conciergerie, Châtelet, and the massive, mock-medieval police headquarters on the Ile de la Cité. To the west, the gorgeous Académie Française by Levau, the Louvre, the domes of the Grand Palais, and the Eiffel Tower. And if the habit of dallying on bridges grows on you, try the **Pont des Arts** some other night; benches have thoughtfully been installed so you can drink in the scenery and anything else you have on hand, all night long. The most romantic bridge is perhaps the **Pont Alexandre III**, linking the Grand Palais on the right bank to Les Invalides on the left. Entered past gilded statues on both banks, the bridge looks as if it were furnished from a Belle Epoque jewelry box, with cherubs squirming under elegant wrought-iron lamps with frosted panes.

Museums... Solitude is the perfect circumstance for viewing art, which is why hearing the parquet creak as you cross an empty gallery is one of the most luxurious experiences you can have in a Parisian museum. To obtain it, or at least to avoid the sweat-suited masses, you should resort to the cover of darkness for museumgoing in Paris. Parisians become singlemindedly interested in dinner from 8pm onward, so you'll often find that you have whole galleries to yourself, an optimum situation for contemplating a favorite canvas or statue, or discovering a new one. Two museums that are especially wonderful at night are the **Musée d'Orsay** and the **Musée Carnavalet**. The Musée d'Orsay is one of the more ingenious architectural projects ever completed in Paris. Italian architect Gae Aulenti brilliantly succeeded in converting an unused train station into a museum for 19th-century art. This is where all of the Impressionists' works are housed, along with a superb collection of work by the Romantics, Realists, Surrealists, and Pointillists (tel 40 49 48 14; 1, rue de Bellechasse, 75007; Métro Solferino; closed Monday, open Thursday until 9:45pm). It also has enchanting views of the illuminated bridges spanning the Seine. The nighttime quiet awakens the real atmosphere of the two magnificent *hôtels*—one Renaissance, one 17th-century—that house the **Musée Carnavalet**. The Hôtel de Sévigné, where Madame de Sévigné lived from 1677 to 1696, covers the city's history from the 16th century to the present, while the adjoining Hôtel Le Peletier de Saint-Fargeau houses Gallo-Roman and Medieval displays (tel 42 72 21 13; 23, rue de Sévigné, 75003; Métro Saint-Paul; closed Monday, open Thursday until 8:30pm.).

Evenings will also let you better experience the magnificence and munificence of what many consider to be the world's greatest museum, the **Musée du Louvre**. Unless you're a glutton who eats a whole pint of ice cream in a single sitting, the best way of approaching this feast is by savoring little spoonfuls, and the museum's late-opening hours are a boon if you decide to take this approach (tel 40 20 50 50/general information, 40 20 51 51/recorded information; Cour Napoléon, 75001; Métro Palais Royale–Musée du Louvre. Closed Tuesday. Aile Richelieu open Monday until 9:45pm, entire museum open Wednesday until 9:45pm). Blockbuster shows such as recent popular exhibitions of Caillebotte and Cézanne usually hang at **Le Grand Palais**, a graceful building with signature greenhouse domes prominent on the low Paris skyline. It was built for the Universal Exhibition of 1900 and subsequently converted to gallery space (tel 44 13 17 17; 3, av. du General Eisenhower, 75008; Métro Champs-Elysées-Clemenceau. Open daily, Wednesday until 10pm).

Four other museums worth your time also have late hours. **Maison Européenne de la Photographie** is a new space and a fantastic addition to the cultural landscape of Paris. Occupying the magnificent mansion Henault de Cantobre, which was built in 1706 and completely renovated to accommodate the museum, it holds a permanent collection of 12,000 photographs taken since 1958 by photographers worldwide. Everything in the collection can be viewed on-screen at 24 work stations in the museum's library (tel 44 78 75 00; 5/7, rue de Fourcy, 75004; Métro Saint-Paul. Open Wednesday through Sunday 11am–8pm). Formerly one of the most beloved museums in the world, the **Jeu de Paume** housed the finest Impressionist collections in France before they were moved to the Musée d'Orsay. This small, neo-Roman temple in the northwest corner of the Tuileries Gardens has since been renovated into a charming venue for contemporary art (tel 47 03 12 50; Jardins des Tuileries, place de la Concorde entrance, 75001; Métro Concorde. Open daily, Tuesday until 9:30pm). The **Musée d'Art Moderne de la Ville de Paris** was originally erected as the pavilion promoting electricity at the Universal Exhibition of 1937, but now this art-moderne building houses the city's municipal collection of modern art, including works by a variety of Cubists. Don't miss Dufy's mural *Electricité*, which was executed for the building (tel 47 23 61 27; 11, av. du President Wilson, 75116; Métro Iena. Closed Monday. Open Wednesday until 8:30pm). Finally, there's the **Musée de Cluny**, an appropriately medieval-looking building that was once the home of the Bishops of Cluny. Bits and pieces of the Gallo-Roman baths that it was built upon are visible at the corner of the boulevards Saint Germain and Saint Michel. As a museum today, it's renowned for its *Lady and the Unicorn* tapestries and other intriguing medieval artifacts (tel 43 25 61 91; 6, place Paul-Painlevé, 75005; Métro Cluny-La Sorbonne).

Art lessons... Unless you speak some French, you'll probably be in over your head here, but if you *parlez assez bien* and would like to indulge in some instructed sketching from live models in an attractive atelier with a professional art teacher, this could be the most fascinating (and French) experience you'll ever have. Run by artist and art teacher Jacques Fivel, the **Académie Fivel** (tel 43 39 12 41; 18, rue Stendahl, 75020; Métro Porte de Bagnolet; courses offered daily except Sunday from 8pm–1am) is a serious and popular school, so you'll have to reserve a place rather than just show up. After the posing session is over, everyone eats something hearty like stew, drinks a lot of red wine, discusses their drawings, and hangs out.

For adults only... For any Frenchman or French woman not satisfied with their spouse or their *cinq à sept*, or 5pm to 7pm as regular after-work liaisons are known, the city offers a variety of other erotic distractions. A lot of them are pretty sleazy, while others add to local color. The Bois de Boulogne, the big park on the western edge of the city, for example, turns into sort of an open-air sex bazaar at night, with such a highly specialized, usually for-pay range of erotic encounters that a Japanese publisher recently brought out a detailed map to help punters from Tokyo find their way to the very spot where Brazilian transsexuals with latex fetishes can be found. Similarly, the *peripherique*, or inner beltway that encircles the city, offers a stunning array of rare local fauna after dark, while boy toys for various purposes congregate around the Trocadero and the Porte Dauphine.

Judging by the enormous number of such places advertised in the back of the weekly entertainment guide *Pariscope*, Parisians would also seem to be very keen on couples-only clubs, as well as other places that are open to the single swinger. One of the best known is the imaginatively named **Deux Plus Deux**, in the Latin Quarter (tel 47 07 25 81; 70, rue Lhomond, 75005; Métro Monge; open daily from noon to dawn). The couples who frequent this well-established club are not here to play cards, which is why only couples are admitted. The complex includes a bar, a discotheque, a restaurant, and a couple of cozy corners where people retreat to recite poetry to one another. The city also has six or seven well-frequented gay bath houses, the most popular of which are the **Key West Sauna** (tel 45 26 31 74; 141, rue Lafayette, 75010; Métro Gare du Nord; open daily until 1am; admission 90F) and the **IDM** (45 23 10 03; 4, rue du Faubourg-Montmartre, 75009; Métro Rue Montmartre; open daily until 1am). Key West Sauna is a busy, American-style gay sauna with a swimming pool, gym, and solarium—hence, perhaps, the name? It's clean and has a diverse clientele, including soldiers on leave. IDM has two floors of frisky fun, plus a gym, sauna, steamroom, and snack bar.

Prefer to play by yourself? Don't despair. When the French government first put the country on line with Minitel service ten years ago, it never occurred to anyone that this very basic interactive information service, designed by France Telecom to replace paper phone books, would eventually vastly broaden the erotic possibilities available to the man or woman on the street. No one really minds, though, since these *lignes rose*, or pink lines, have become a lucrative source of revenue. Most hotels and all most offices have Minitel terminals, which are designed like very simple computers, and most of the vast number of erotic lines begin with the prefix 3615 followed by a specific number. While some lines will put you in touch with pay-to-play services, most of them work like electronic personal ads. You may see advertisements for one of the most popular lines, 3615 CUM, in the Métro. You get the idea.

Browsing... Rumbling stomach? Paris is not an especially wonderful late-night shopping city, but diehard night people can usually scare up the vital necessities. As in most major American cities, some of the big department stores stay open late on Thursdays. **Au Printemps** (tel 42 82 50 00; 64, bd. Haussmann, 75009; Métro Havre-Caumartin; open Thursday until 10pm) is among the biggies of Parisian department stores and is know for being the most fashion-aggressive. Come here in search of that breaking, little-known designer who hasn't yet been scooped up by Barneys in the U.S. The place to look is the department called *la rue à la mode*. The store also sells kitchenware, china, and a variety of other possible gift items. **Galeries Lafayette** (tel 42 82 34 56; 40, bd. Haussmann, 75009; Métro Chaussee D'Antin; open

Thursday until 10pm) is the archrival of Printemps and is a beret-toss away. This grande dame also carries an impressive range of fashion, as well as household goods, cosmetics, perfumes, and home linens. Check out its own label clothing, the *Avant Première* line, which is a changing selection of styles that have been inspired by the very latest looks on Paris runways.

For cigarette smokers... Smokers, be forewarned that cigs are only sold at *tabacs*, usually within cafés, and most of them close at around 9pm. If you're caught short, head for **Le Jean Bart** (86, rue de Rivoli, 75004; open until 2am during the week, midnight on the weekends), **Tabac Le Marigny** (43, rue de Charonne, 75011; Métro Charonne; open until 11pm), **Tabac du Matin** (12, bd. Poissonière, 75009; Métro Rue Montmartre; open daily until 11:45pm) or **La Havane**, a real godsend (4, place de Clichy, 75017; Métro Place de Clichy; open daily until 4am, reopens at 6:30am).

Clothing... Shrewd shoppers adore *Prisunic* (tel 42 25 27 46; 109, rue de la Boétie, 75008; Métro Franklin-D.-Roosevelt; open Monday through Saturday until midnight), a cheap and cheerful chain store that sells trendy, inexpensive clothing under its *Miss Helen* label. Look also for *Bourjois* cosmetics, which are made in the same factory that produces Chanel's face paints. The store also stocks a whole rubbish bin worth of deliriously tacky souvenirs along the lines of T-shirts that say, "Dad got a hand job in Paris. All I got was this tacky T-shirt." If everyone's already seen your orange plush pullover and you're a cool guy desperate for some trendy new clubwear, beam on over to **Boy's Bazaar** until midnight. The store carries a whole range of way-trendy lines from Katherine Hamnett to Vent Couvert (tel 42 71 94 00; 5, rue Sainte-Croix-de-la-Bretonnerie, 75004; Métro Hôtel-de-Ville; open noon–midnight, except Sunday 2–9).

Groceries after hours... **Chez Salem** (tel 46 06 60 03; 20, bd. de Clichy, 75018; Métro Pigalle; closed Monday) is a tiny grocery store in the Pigalle party district that stays open 24 hours and sells beer and wine round the clock. **Layrac** (tel 43 25 17 72; 29, rue de Buci, 75006; Métro Odéon; open Monday through Thursday until midnight, Friday and Saturday until 1am, Sunday until 11pm) is a gorgeous catering store and a perfect place to pick up the makings of a first-class picnic or cold supper. The store also sells water, wine, and other booze, and is pricey but worth it. Seeking something a little classier than a quick bite at McDonald's or one of the other fast-food places on the Champs-Elysées? Stop at **La Maison de Cavier** for the finest Iranian caviar, plus a range of smoked fish and vodkas (tel 47 23 53 43; 1, rue Vernet, 75008; Métro George-V; open daily until 1am). **Noura** is a wonderful option if you want a night off from French food and feel like holing up in your hotel. This elegant caterer does all of the wealthy local Lebanese community's parties and sells excellent platters of *mezze* (mixed hors d'oeuvres), salads, shish kebab, sticky baklava, and wine (tel 47 23 02 20; 27, av. Marceau, 75016; Métro Iena; open daily until midnight). **Boulangerie de l'Ancienne Comédie** is a bakery and vital address for dedicated noctambulists, especially if you've been out late playing on the Left Bank. The boulangerie not only does bread and croissants for tomorrow morning, but also sandwiches, quiches, and pizza (tel 43 26 89 72; 10, rue de l'Ancienne Comédie, 75006; Métro Odéon; open Monday through Saturday 24 hours). **La Grande Epicerie de Paris** (tel 44 39 81 00; 38, rue de Sèvres, 75007; Métro Sèvres-Babylone; open daily until 9pm) is the grocery store annex of the tony Le Bon Marché department store and one of the most dazzling places to shop for food in Paris. Here you'll ogle at fantastic displays and a huge selection of rare oils, teas, honeys, preserves, vinegars, and cheeses. This is an ideal stop for your own kitchen back home or for gifts. **Prisunic** (tel 42 25 27 46; 109, rue de la Boétie, 75008; Métro Franklin-D.-Roosevelt; open Monday through Saturday until midnight) may have earned its rep as a clothing store, but the basement sells prepared salads, cheese, cold cuts, bread, wine, and water. If you're scouting for picnic food, this is the place.

Condoms... One of the largest and most unusual selections of life preservers found anywhere in the world is on display at **Condoms** (tel 43 29 07 89; 14, rue de l'Ancienne Comédie, 75006; Métro Odéon; open Monday through Thursday until 11pm, Friday and Saturday until 1am).

There are little raincoats here in a wide selection of flavors, fragrances, and textures. In addition, the store also sells various other sensual aids like massage oils and lubricants.

Gas... Rolling into town in the dead of night on empty? **Essence 24/h** is open nonstop (338, rue Saint-Honoré, 75002).

Browsing for books... La Hune has the reputation as one of the best and chicest bookstores in Paris. It carries an especially good assortment of art books and other coffee-table tomes. As good for star-spotting as it is for browsing because a lot of famous, always-in-dark-glasses types come by late at night (tel 45 48 35 85; 170, bd. Saint-Germain, 75006; Métro Saint-Germain-des-Prés; open Monday through Saturday until 11:45pm). Founded by American expatriate Sylvia Beach, who published James Joyce's *Ulysses,* **Shakespeare & Company** (tel 43 26 96 50; 37, rue de la Bûcherie, 75005; Métro Maubert-Mutualité; open daily until midnight) is a jam-packed little shop, and though it's a reasonable place to root around for something to read on the train or various English books that haven't yet made it to North America, don't expect your dreams of *les Années Folles* to be realized.

Browsing for newspapers and magazines... Insomniacs desperate for something to read can cab it over to the kiosk on the **Place Pigalle** (Métro Pigalle; open 24 hours daily, except on Sunday nights). The kiosk at the corner of the **rue de Faubourg-Montmartre** and the **boulevard Montmartre** is open 24 hours a day for newspapers, guides, magazines, and the odd assortment of stuff that kiosks stock. Also on hand are urban life's other vital necessities, like cigarettes and condoms, at prices that desperation will command.

Music... Virgin Megastore (tel 49 53 50 00; 52–60, av. des Champs-Elysées, 75008; Métro Franklin-D.-Roosevelt; open Monday through Thursday and Sunday until midnight, until 1am on Friday and Saturday) was opened by British cool-guy tycoon Richard Branson. It's his first beachhead in France, and it's been a big success. Come here for good prices on CDs, cassettes, videos, and electronic equipment. Quite a social scene, too; the average age is about 20. If you know what you're after already and don't want to tackle the gigantic Virgin Megastore up the street, you can hurriedly nip in and out of **Champs Disques** for a new CD or cassette (tel 45 62 65 46; 84, av. des Champs-Elysées, 75008; Métro Franklin-D.-Roosevelt; open Monday through Saturday until midnight).

Sundries and such... One of the great institutions of the Paris night, **Le Drugstore** is sort of a mini-mall, with counters selling everything from S. T. Dupont pens to Patricia Kass CDs. This particular branch (tel 47 23 54 34; 133, av. des Champs-Elysées, 75008; Métro Etoile; open daily until 2am) attracts a very funky and frisky crowd of night people. Note that if you once frequented their Saint-Germain branch, it's now closed. To the fury of people in that neighborhood, it's slated to become an Emporio Armani.

late nigh

dining

No matter what time you
surface from a jet-lagged
nap, a steamy disco, or
some amorous ardors in
your hotel room, part of
the privilege of being in
Paris is tumbling into a

cab and setting off for a good late-night feed. Despite skidding culinary standards caused by fast food, microwave ovens, and industrially prepared ingredients, Paris remains the uncontested after-hours culinary capital of the west.

Though none of the city's temples to haute cuisine stays open past 10:30, Paris offers a splendid selection of late-night and after-hours meals that are blissful light years ahead of the omelet-and-rye-toast fare you may be reduced to after midnight back home. The most popular choices right now are the baby bistros. Launched by top chefs such as Guy Savoy because of the recession, these are casual, gently priced satellites of the more famous and expensive restaurants bearing their names. Several of Guy Savoy's restaurants, including Les Bookinistes, La Butte Chaillot and Le Cap Vernet, serve quite late, affording even late-night diners a chance to experience excellent contemporary bistro cooking.

Etiquette

Even if you're planning to gorge yourself on oysters at 2am, it's still a good idea to call and reserve before just showing up. Late-night dining *is* popular in Paris, and during certain major trade fairs, these night-owl haunts can be crowded.

In terms of clothing, you can get away with jeans in most of the restaurants I recommend, but men should wear jackets even if ties aren't necessary. You'll find in general, however, that you'll be better seated and served if you take even a little trouble with your appearance. Whatever you do, ditch the sneakers, don't wear shorts anywhere in Paris at night, and don't bring luggage to a restaurant (all the train stations have baggage-checking facilities).

You obviously have every right to eat whatever you please, but you should remember that there are still major differences between French and North American eating habits. The French wouldn't dream of drinking hard liquor, coffee, or soda with a meal, and diet drinks are almost never available. Wine and water are the libations of choice, and if you're watching your pennies, skip bottled water, which, for a half bottle, runs about four dollars in most restaurants. Ask instead for a *carafe d'eau*, or carafe of tap water. If you don't know much about wine, you're probably best off with one of the house wines, which are generally reliable. Fish is usually served on the bone and meat is cooked rare to very rare; ask for yours *bien cuit*, or well-done, if you prefer it otherwise. Though it's starting to change some, especially with the current popularity of Mediterranean cooking, Parisians consider vegetables to be a bore, so have a salad for lunch in a cafe if you're craving greenery—it's not likely to show up on a dinner menu. Try not to fret fat, salt, butter, sugar, or any of the other contemporary stateside dietary preoccupations while you're in Paris; you're on vacation and you might note that you only rarely see overweight people here—food for thought, *n'est-ce pas?* Need some mustard? Never call a waiter "garçon"; the polite way to request a server's attention is to say, "*S'il vous plaît*" ("If you please"). Finally, the French do not drink capuccino. In fact, they only drink coffee with milk in the morning; if you want yours with milk, ask for a *café crème*, and be prepared for a smirk… you can always smirk back.

If you're in town only for a few days and want to get the very best of Paris late dining, hit one of the glamorous brasseries (see "Metropolitan glamour," below), do a Guy Savoy bistro (see "Gourmet eating at odd hours," below), or try one of the old-fashioned, late-night bistros around Les Halles (see "For local color," below). The odds are good that your memories of the *plateau de fruits de mer* (tray of mixed shellfish) at Le Vaudeville or your massive *côte de boeuf* (rib of beef) at La Tour Montlhery will last for years to come.

For local color... If there's one nonstop that everyone goes crazy for, it's **La Tour Montlhery**, a bawdy old-fashioned bistro on the edge of the ugly subterranean shopping center that is Les Halles today. This place still retains a bit of the bluff working-man's character it had in the days when it served robust meals to vendors and porters in the food market that Zola called the "belly of Paris." Though not really a place to whisper sweet nothings into one another's ears—it's noisy, smoky, and clamorous—you'll love the atmosphere, the house wines are very good, and they do one of the best *côtes de boeuf* (rib steaks) for two in town.

A few blocks away is **La Poule au Pot**, a charming old place that serves a delectable version of the classic French dish for which it is named—hen stewed in its own broth, with potatoes and vegetables, perfect hangover food—along with other sturdy bistro dishes, to a spirited and motley assortment of nightbirds.

Round the clock... On the edge of Les Halles, along the rue Coquillière, are two of the city's most venerable 24-hour brasseries, **Au Pied de Cochon** and **L'Alsace aux Halles**. If their menus are similar, their atmospheres are planets apart. Au Pied de Cochon has a theatrical decor, including huge bunch-of-grapes wall sconces, and attracts a party crowd, while L'Alsace is perfect if you want crisp linens, calm, and the occasional distraction of a bit of Alsatian kitsch. The **Chez Clement** chain, with branches on the Champs-Elysées and near the Opéra, offers a surprisingly appetizing chain-restaurant take on the bistro and is open 24 hours a day. You might describe it as the Gallic version of Denny's or Howard Johnson's. **Aux Perroquets** is another all-night option in Les Halles, serving simple fare to everyone from local butchers starting the day to club kids just winding down.

In search of art nouveau and oysters... For many people, sumptuous art nouveau decor and big trays of freshly opened oysters on crushed ice are essential emblems of Paris. Find both at **Julien** and the **Brasserie Flo**, which both attract a stylish clientele, including many who work in the fashion industry. Flo is the rowdier and more easygoing of the pair, while Julien is so magnificent that your memories of it will sustain you through more than a few dreary days. If you're planning to propose to someone, or to celebrate an anniversary, Julien would be a superb backdrop. The food at both places is quite good, too. Note, by the way, that many of the stay-open-late brasseries are owned by the Brasserie Flo chain, including not just these two, but **La Coupole**, **Le Vaudeville** and **Le Boeuf sur la Toit**. The Flo family generally offers a quality feed in handsome settings with a stylish crowd, but if you're only in Paris for a few days you might not want to repeat what is essentially the same menu.

Metropolitan glamour... **La Coupole**, the most famous brasserie in the world and a place that's synonymous with Montparnasse is a fabulous scene with at least 20 nationalities strutting their idea of being dressed to the nines every night. The painted columns, each one done by a different artist in the twenties; the champagne corks popping; the huge, almost surreal-looking trays of shellfish arranged on beds of crushed ice like fine jewelry on velvet—this is one of the great experiences of the Paris night and suits almost any occasion you might invent. You can happily spend an evening tarrying over a meal at **Le Telegraphe**, which is very sophisticated without being stuffy. Though this is a restaurant, it has a real night feel to it, and the bar's a great place to linger before or after dinner. Press attachés from the big Paris fashion houses love this place because the service is good and the tables generously spaced. It draws a very attractive and well-dressed crowd.

For someplace a bit more Parisian and more chic by local standards, try **Le Boeuf sur la Toit**, the proverbial little-black-dress of the city's brasseries, understated but jaw-droppingly beautiful. It's a favored haunt of French film stars, media people, German tourists, and industrialists with beautiful young women who probably aren't their daughters. You'll get a deep dose of contemporary Parisian style during at this dressy and overwhelmingly wonderful place to stroll through the door at 11pm. The brilliant seafood at **Paul Minchelli** has made this another one of the city's hottest restaurants, and the elegant interior doesn't hurt either. The decor is simpler at **Le Bamboche**, but the quality of the food—updated French regional classics—is just as high.

Tête-à-tête... So Paris got into your blood and you went back to the hotel and split a bottle of champagne and had a better romp together than you've had in ages. Don't just sit there on the bed in your bathrobes watching CNN. Keep the love light burning by going to **Le Vaudeville**, an intimate art-deco brasserie where you can have some more champagne, some oysters, some foie gras, and show off your good mood. You can be certain that the crowd here will know what you've been up to. Or else maybe you'll surprise yourself and yearn to go somewhere that's deeply traditional to the point of being almost fogeyish. Quiet and dignified, **La Cloche d'Or** is the classic late feed for journalists and theater people; white tablecloths, a distinguished wine list, and career waiters give it a decidedly grown-up feel, and the simple food's pretty good, too.

Only in Paris—high-voltage scenes... **Natacha**, in Montparnasse, blazes with high-voltage starlight nightly until 1am. As is true of many such places, you probably won't understand what makes it so special. Neither the food nor the decor is particularly alluring, but this doesn't dissuade everyone from Cher to Gérard Depardieu to Mickey Rourke from hanging out here.

A more genuine party will take place around your table at the absolutely fabulous **Chez Omar** on the northern edge of the trendy Marais district. Everyone loves Omar, a genial, generous Algerian who once worked at La Coupole. Omar, in turn, loves everyone, including painters, Vivienne Westwood and other fashion designers, photographers, journalists—in short, the whole Paris beau monde. His couscous is excellent, too, and he has a solid list of very fairly priced Bordeaux.

In a Helmut Newton state of mind... The famed German photographer has often used the luxurious decors of Paris's grand hotels as gilded-cage backgrounds for his sometimes rather harshly erotic tableaux. If it amuses you to pick up the sensual scent implicit in these fabled palaces, try a late supper at **Le Relais Plaza**, a stunning art-deco dining room in the *soigné* Plaza Athenée Hotel. Although terribly chic, it has no scene, per se, but the ambience is the very definition of *la vie en rose*. In other words, it's a perfect place to be wearing wildly sexy and expensive underwear under a Jil Sander pants suit. Oh, and the food's good, too.

Gourmet eating at odd hours... Guy Savoy is one of the most innovative restaurateurs in Paris, and his bistro annexes—the restaurants he's opened in search of a larger audience than comes to his eponymous Michelin two-star—serve excellent food in stylish surroundings to youngish, lively crowds. If you're clubbing schedule has you out of synch with regular meal hours, or if you don't want to be pinned down to a reservation but like to eat well, **La Butte Chaillot**, **Le Cap Vernet** and **Les Bookinistes** are invaluable addresses. Reservations can, and should, be made at the last minute, and you'll have a chance to sample some of the best contemporary bistro cooking in Paris. If you don't know what this might mean, think French comfort food like roast chicken with potato puree or a tuna steak with ratatouille.

Where the boys are... Fashionable Paris loves dining late, and beyond the appealing democracy of the brasseries, each of the city's nocturnal tribes has its favorite spots. The *dernier cri* of late-night noshing is **Yvan sur Seine**, a snug little bistro on the quai du Louvre just across from the Seine. The pun in the restaurant's name tells all—it means "Yvan on the Seine," and in French, "Seine" and "scene" are pronounced the same. The streaked-blond Belgian-Czech Yvan, an excellent chef, is also something of a party boy, and he's opened this annex as a canteen for his friends, many of whom are gay couples. They serve until 4am. The crowd evolves as the night goes on, generally anchored by stylish groups of late-thir-tysomething friends.

See-and-be-scenes... If you're as interested in a good show as you are in eating well, stop by the **Café Marly** in the Cour Napoléon du Louvre. Almost everything that comes out at night comes through here sooner or later, and the cafe serves a generically trendy menu—moz-zarella and tomato salad, smoked salmon, cheese-filled ravioli—until 2am.

The fact that film director Roman Polanski is a reg-ular at **Barfly** on the avenue George V says it all about this red-hot, year-old restaurant-bar. Not surprisingly, given his patronage, a bevy of models in short black dresses, along with a whole *Paris Match*-full of people who are *mediatique* (frequently photographed), come here for indifferent food until 2am.

Pre- and post-club grazing grounds... Friendly and low-key, Claude Aurensan's **La Maison**, on a tiny little street in the Latin Quarter, is an ideal place to rev up a club mood. Aurensan used to work at Le Palace, the big seventies boom-boom disco, and his following includes a spicy mix of good-looking boys in motorcycle jackets, along with famous actresses like Catherine Deneuve and Leslie Caron. During the summer, you sit out on one of the best terraces in Paris—there's no traffic and several trees—and the food's better than might be expected at such a stylish spot. After clubbing there's **Le Depanneur**, a sort of brash, American-style diner on the edges of the Place Pigalle. It pulls an interesting mixture of club hounds and exotic fauna to nibble on salads and burgers, over a last drink that's as endless as you'd like it to be because the place is open 24 hours. For casting, think *Wild at Heart* and *Desperately Seeking Susan*.

Animal house... The **Pub Saint Germain**, known to back-packers from around the world, is the classic moderately priced *address de nuit* at the end of a crawl through the adjacent Latin Quarter. Don't let the closed metal gates put you off—you have to ring for admittance to what's a veritable Ali Baba's cave for beer lovers. Are you starving, but nearly broke from a night of pricey club life? The Boulangerie de l'Ancienne Comédie, across the street from the Pub Saint Germain, sells fresh bread, croissants, pizzas, and sandwiches all night long.

Foreign affairs... Paris can also satisfy a variety of ethnic cravings in the wee hours. **Da Bettega** serves credible pasta to well-soused jazz hounds and also undecided couples who've at least gotten as far as leaving Castel's, the oh-so-exclusive club a block over. A real and sometimes wonderful collection of unself-conscious oddballs finds their way to the **Palais de l'Est**, which is not a palace at all, but a simple Chinese-Vietnamese place not far from two major train stations, and it happens to serve until 5am. Think young cadets worrying about being AWOL over baby eggrolls, nightclub personnel, cab drivers, dubiously triumphant poets, a crowd that would make Henry Miller proud.

The Index

$$$$	more than 300F	more than $60
$$$	200F–300F	$40–$60
$$	100F–200F	$20–$40
$	Less than 100F	less than $20

Prices are per person, not including drinks.

L'Alsace aux Halles. Old-fashioned service and a dose of Alsatian kitsch are an appealing combination at this venerable brasserie on the north edge of Les Halles. A fine place for a feast of oysters and other shellfish from the crushed-ice-filled stand out front. It also does a very good *choucroute garni*—the Alsatian classic of mild sauerkraut covered with sausage and various cuts of pork—and grilled fish and steaks. Though it's usually lively enough, this is a good address if your partner's more important than your surroundings, and you want to eat well.... *Tel 42 36 74 24; 16, rue Coquilliere, 75001. Métro Les Halles. Open 24 hours. $$*

Aux Perroquets. Located in Les Halles, which used to be the city's major wholesale food market, this all-night restaurant serves simple dishes such as onion soup to a varied crowd of laborers, partiers and insomniacs.... *Tel 42 36 37 26; 84, rue Saint–Honoré, 75001; Métro Louvre. Open 9pm–8am. Closed one week in Aug. AE not accepted. $*

Le Bamboche. Young chef David Van Laer displays his talent in his simply decorated restaurant. Updated classics include lentil soup with escargots, veal fillet with walnut cream, and *hachis parmentier* (shepherd's pie) with blood sausage.... *Tel 45 49 14 40; 15, rue de Babylone, 75007; Métro Sèvres-Babylone. Closed Sat and Sun. $$$*

Barfly. Novelist Charles Bukowski would not recognize the crowd in the bar that his novel inspired. Long-legged beauties and lupine playboys mix it up with a French movie and theater crowd, spiked by the odd (*sic*) party personality. You come here to preen as much as to eat and drink, and though some might find the whole show a tad pretentious, it's fun if viewed from a distance. Note that reservations are essential because of a capricious door policy favoring the handsome, beautiful, and famous.... *Tel 53 67 84 60; 49, av. George V, 75008; Métro Alma-Marceau. Open daily noon–3pm, 7:30pm–2am. $$*

Da Bettega. This snug Italian place is a de facto annex of Castel's, the aristocratic granddaddy of Paris clubs just up the street, and the crowd tends to wordly gents with recently met Lolitas, couples not unlike the duo Princess Caroline of Monaco formed running around town with former first husband Philippe Junot. The atmosphere's friendly but a bit clubby, and you get the feeling that the food on neighboring tables was more often ordered as a prop to a looming decision about where to end the night than as a needed meal. Still, the pasta's good, and this is a reasonable bet in Saint Germain, regardless of where you've been beforehand.... *Tel 43 29 97 37; 4, rue Princess, 75006; Métro Mabillon. Open daily 8pm–5am. AE, DC not accepted. $$*

Le Boeuf sur le Toit. For a drop-dead glamorous setting, this art-deco brasserie is the place. The well-lit dining room has soaring mirrored walls, banks of ferns, big geometric deco chandeliers, and an appealingly naughty buzz. Frequented by French film stars and show-biz types, it's a *soigné* spot at which to splurge on a massive tray of cold shellfish, including oysters, shrimps, langoustines, and lobster. If you want something earthier, the cassoulet's quite good.... *Tel 43 59 83 80; 34, rue du Colisée, 75008; Métro Saint-Philippe-du-Roule. Open daily noon–2am. $$$*

Les Bookinistes. Chef Guy Savoy has demonstrated an extraordinary aptitude for creating restaurants that unfailingly cater to the tastes of contemporary Parisians (see also **Le Cap Vernet** and **La Butte Chaillot**). His first Left Bank venture, Les Boookinistes, opened two years ago, and has become extremely popular with a sophisticated local crowd. Art and antique dealers, book publishers, and fashion people love to dine at all hours on the eclectic but delicious modern bistro food served in a jaunty, postmodern dining room overlooking the Seine. Whether you're dining late or not, this place is definitely worth a meal during your Paris visit. *Tel 43 25 45 94; 53, quai des Grands-Augustins, 75006; Métro Saint-Michel. Open Mon–Fri noon–2:30pm, 7pm–midnight; Sat 7pm–midnight.* $$$

La Butte Chaillot. Not only the decor but the crowd are reminiscent of similar new-wave brasseries in Los Angeles, New York, and London. Think cool chic, as in, respectively, terracotta-colored walls, a glass staircase, turquoise leather chairs, designer sunglasses, Prada backpacks, and cellular phones. The menu is a study in what fashionable Parisians like to eat these days, including tiny cheese ravioli, rotisserie chicken with pureed potatoes and stuffed veal breast. A good choice if you want stylish surroundings but not a noisy scene.... *Tel 47 27 88 88; 110 bis, av. Kleber, 75016; Métro Trocadero. Open daily noon–2:30pm, 7pm–12:30am. DC, MC not accepted.*$$

Brasserie Flo. One of the most boisterous and beautiful brasseries in Paris with a stunning art nouveau interior. This place is a particular favorite of Parisians, which gives it an extra dose of *vie en rose* atmosphere. A good choice when you're in a gregarious mood or want to be surrounded by one. Order the house specialty of *choucroute garni* only if you're ravenous, because the vast mound of mild sauerkraut studded with sausage and pork and accompanied by boiled potatoes requires a brawny appetite. More decorously, the grilled fish and meats are excellent, as is the foie gras.... *Tel 47 70 13 59; 7, cour des Petites-Ecuries, 75010; Métro Château d'Eau. Open daily noon–3pm, 7pm–1am.* $$$

Le Café Marly. The latest venture of the trend-alert Costes brothers, this place has a dramatic Napoleon III decor with Pompeiian red walls and black trim. Though the food's rather ordinary, it's one of the chicest late-night scenes in Paris, with a high eye-contact factor. Best of all, its location in the courtyard of the Louvre means that it offers spectacular views of the illuminated I. M. Pei pyramid from its terrace at night. Perfect for a light meal after a stroll in the newly renovated Tuileries gardens.... *Tel 49 26 06 60; 93, rue de Rivoli, Cour Napoleon du Louvre, 75001; Métro Palais-Royal. Open daily 11am–1am. AE, DC, MC not accepted.* $$

Le Cap Vernet. Guy Savoy's first venture into brasseries has become a popular late-night haunt for those heading on to L'Arc, the Queen, or Barfly. The bilevel dining room has a sophisticated yachting theme, with a lot of chrome, blue leather, and well-polished tropical wood, and the lighting is especially discreet. A fine place for a light meal, with starters like an excellent arugula and main courses such as sole meunière. The crowd runs to young execs in jeans and blazers and blond babes of various ages.... *Tel 47 20 20 04; 82, av. Marceau, 75008; Métro Etoile. Open daily 9am–midnight. DC not accepted.* $$

Chez Clement. The eclectic decor of this chain bistro looks rather as though it might have been done by Disney, but the pastiche is harmless; with its easy prices and good food, this place is very popular. Splash out on a tray of oysters and then go with one of the rotisseried meats, all of which are served on an all-you-can-eat basis.... *Tel 40 73 87 00; 123, av. Champs-Elysées, 75008; Métro George-V. Open 24 hours daily. AE, DC not accepted.* $$

Chez Omar. A meal at this handsome Belle Epoque bistro turned North African restaurant is sort of like being invited to a private party. The lively, friendly crowd—many of whom are artists, photographers, or fashion types—the bustle of the waiters, and the omnipresent solicitude of smiling anglophone proprietor Omar Guerida light up the room nightly. Many Parisians also feel this place serves the best couscous in town. For those with more conventional palates, first-rate grilled steaks and lamb chops are also offered. *Tel 42 72 36 26; 47, rue de Bretagne, 75003; Métro Filles du Calvaire. Open Mon–Sat noon–3pm, 7:30pm–midnight; Sun noon–midnight. No credit cards.* $$

La Cloche d'Or. A rather mature and resolutely French crowd of journalists, theater owners, and actors fill this intriguingly old-fashioned place every evening. Something in its calm rituals will make you feel grown-up, too. Some of this monument's customers have come to the same table nightly for thirty years. The reason you should know about it is not that the food's particularly brilliant, but because it offers a solid feed in quiet surroundings in a clamorous neighborhood—along with a dollop of authentic Paris charm. Stick with a steak and maybe a bottle of Bordeaux from the distinguished wine list.... *Tel 48 74 48 88; 3, rue Mansart, 75009; Métro Blanche. Open Mon–Sat 7pm–5am. $$$*

La Coupole. Don't come to this sprawling brasserie in the hopes of catching a whiff of Lost Generation Paris. Very few artists could afford the menu here today, and they've largely been replaced by a well-heeled international crowd of tourists and business people—with a few top-drawer French intellectuals to spice the mix. Part of the Brasserie Flo chain since 1988, it's a pleasant place to scarf down a tray of oysters and some grilled sole. The service gets better as it gets later and less crowded.... *Tel 43 20 14 20; 102, bd. du Montparnasse; Métro Vavin. Open daily noon–3pm, 7pm–1:30am. $$$*

Le Depanneur. This ersatz, American-style diner serves drinks, salads, sandwiches, and attitude round the clock. The super-cool young crowd—men in motorcycle jackets and many women with the Pekinese looks of actress Vanessa Paradis pose in the smoky din for hours on end. Good for drinks, if you want one for the road after clubbing around the Place Pigalle.... *Tel 40 16 40 20; 27, rue Fontaine, 75009; Métro Blanche. Open 24 hours daily. AE, DC not accepted. $*

Julien. The art-nouveau splendor of this venerable brasserie is perhaps heightened by the red-light garishness of the surrounding neighborhood. The area's perfectly safe, though, and this branch of the Brasserie Flo group is one of the most atmospheric late-nighters in town, attracting a cross-section of stylish Parisians with its delicious foie gras, salmon, and steaks. Though you won't be turned away in jeans, it's a rather dressier spot than other wee-hour feeds, and a place to come for a meal rather than a snack.... *Tel 47 70 12 06; 16, rue Faubourg St-Denis, 75010; Métro Strasbourg St-Denis. Open daily noon–3pm, 7pm–1:30am. $$$*

La Maison. Even if you don't recognize any of the many local stars who favor this place, you probably appreciate a pretty face. More important, the outdoor terrace here is absolute bliss on a warm night, and the food's pleasant, too. A very popular pre-club rendezvous for night people, there's always a buzz in the intimate little dining room, and no one will chase you away if you suddenly decide on a second bottle of wine at 11:25. The sliced chicken in lemon sauce and steak tartare are especially good.... *Tel 43 29 73 57; 1, rue de la Bûcherie, 75005; Métro Saint-Michel. Open Tues–Sun noon–2:30pm, 7:30–11:30pm. AE, DC not accepted. $$*

Natacha. Rather like a nursery for stars—oh, look, isn't that Johnny Depp?—this is where the biggest names and egos come when they want word to get out that they're in town, but don't want to rub elbows with real hoi polloi. If star-spotting's your game, if you want to observe firsthand whether or not Madonna knows which fork to use, book a table and be sure to act cool. Some French stars pop in occasionally, but the tone of this place is very international. The food's okay, and plenty of fish and vegetables are on the menu in deference to the life-term weight watchers in the crowd.... *Tel 43 20 79 27; 17 bis, rue Campagne-Première, 75014; Métro Raspail. Open Mon–Sat 8:30pm–1am. DC not accepted. $$$*

Palais de l'Est. Aside from reasonably good Chinese, Thai, and Vietnamese food, the crowd here is oddly intriguing in a Jim Jarmusch sort of way. Palais is filled with the con-temporary version of the smudgy-faced stokers and absinthe-sodden streetwalkers that Brassai, Paris's most famous nocturnal photographer, captured during the twen-ties. Who they are and what they're doing eating shrimp in chili sauce in the middle of the night would make a good novel. Not in the least glamorous, this is a good destina-tion for confirmed noctambules and lovers of Asian food. Ask for a table in the more comfortable first-floor dining room.... *Tel 46 07 09 99; 186, rue du Faubourg-Saint-*

Martin, 75010. Open daily 7pm–5am. Métro Gare de l'Est. AE, DC not accepted. $–$$

Paul Minchelli. As chic as Paris dining gets right now. Chef Paul Minchelli, formerly of once-great Le Duc, demonstrates that good fish preparation is about precision in cooking times and seasoning. Try the baby clams with hot peppers and the sea bass. If you're traveling alone, book to eat at the bar.... Tel 47 05 89 86; 54 blvd. de Latour-Maubourg, 75007; Métro Ecole-Militaire. Closed Sun and Mon. AE, D, DC, MC not accepted. $$

Au Pied de Cochon. Though this place has made it into guidebooks in every language known to man, and, sometimes it would seem, beast, the tourist glare enhances rather than diminishes the nightly show here. Don't come for a gourmet feed—you'll eat well enough, and depending on the kitchen, maybe even well—but for the invincible silliness of the scene. The waiters play dumb, but the rugby team from Toulouse, the four tour operators from Bangkok, two exhausted bar hostesses, and a gaggle of American college kids using Mom's for-emergencies-only American Express card all love the daft lighting fixtures, the lobster tank, the brass pig's-feet door handles, the whole shebang. Unless you're mad for pig's feet—a shopworn statistic they provide claims that they serve over 80,000 a year—a perfect meal here is the cheese-topped onion soup followed by the steak tartare washed down with a surprisingly good Beaujolais Rose.... Tel 42 36 11 75; 6, rue Coquilliere, 75001; Métro Les Halles. Open 24 hours daily. $$

La Poule au Pot. Little brass plaques line the wooden railing above the banquettes here, each one engraved with the name of a celebrity client, Santana or the Rolling Stones, for example. This venerable but friendly bistro develops a bit of a party atmosphere as the night goes on, with a diverse crowd of arty Parisian night crawlers seasoned with the odd star. Starlight or not, it's a cozy, consoling spot with pink tulip lamps over the bar and wine-label print wallpaper. The dish from which it takes its name—hen stewed in a rich broth with potatoes, carrots, and celery—is excellent, and the onion soup, sealed in its

ceramic bowl with a runny plug of gruyère cheese is delicious, too. The short and very expensive wine list is the
only obstacle to full-throttle abandon.... *Tel 42 36 32 96;
9, rue Vauvilliers, 75001; Métro Les Halles. Open
Tues–Sun 7pm–6am. AE, DC not accepted. $$$*

Pub Saint Germain. Sometimes there's a whiff of frat-house
frolics in the air at this rollicking anchor of Left Bank
nightlife, but because the place is so enormous, you can
always find a quieter corner if your mood is more sedate.
Though the great selection of beers, including a full array of
Belgian Abbey brews, is a major part of the draw, you can
also get a decent steak with fries or a salad if you need a lit-
tle ballast. Convenient and friendly, it's also a help that they
accept all credit cards if you need to save your last hundred
francs for a cab home afterwards.... *Tel 43 29 38 70; 17,
rue de l'Ancienne-Comédie, 75006; Métro Odéon. Open 24
hours daily. $$*

Le Relais Plaza. Are you an older German woman with an
ardent young Brazilian lover? Or perhaps a sultan keen to
impress a young sparrow who's just alighted in town from
Eastern Europe? One way or another, such duos often form
a part of the intriguing if discreet human scenery at this elegant art-deco dining room in the Hôtel Plaza Athenée. One
of the most stylish places in Paris for lunch, it's also a
delightful place for a dressy late supper. Come for a perfectly
boned grilled sole with fresh *pommes frites* and sautéed
spinach, maybe washed down with a bottle of Mersault or
champagne.... *Tel 47 23 46 36; 21, av. Montaigne,
75008; Métro Champs-Elysées-Clemenceau. Open daily
noon–3pm, 7pm–1:30am. $$$*

La Tour Monthlery. It is a fantastic experience, but this place
takes a little work. For starters, you should come hungry
and you must reserve, even if you call only ten minutes
before you show up. After all, part of the charm here is
that they could basically care less if you come or not. This
doesn't translate to nasty service, it's just that they have
such a loyal local following that they don't depend on your
withered dollars. Having arrived, be patient; they'll get you
to your table, but this place isn't about the niceties you
may be expecting in Paris. Seated at last, skip a starter

PARIS (LATE NIGHT DINING

unless you're famished, in which case the poached eggs in beef aspic with parsley and ham stripes are weirdly neo-*Good-Housekeeping* but delicious. Then share the *côte de boeuf* or gorge yourself on juicy mutton chops. Vegetarians need not apply, and the house wines are the only way to go.... *Tel 42 36 21 82; 5, rue Prouvaires, 75001; Métro Les Halles. Open Mon–Fri 24 hours. AE, DC not accepted. $$*

Le Telegraphe. Housed in a former dormitory for female telephone operators, this rather tony restaurant has a worldly art-deco decor, a charming piano bar, and a tiny interior garden where you can dine outside in good weather. It's a perfect spot if you feel like wearing a little Armani but aren't quite up for anything too grand. The menu is a sort of top-of-the-charts of what fashionable Parisians like to eat these days—tomato and mozzarella salad, grilled veal, lemon tart—appetizing, if not particularly exciting. But who cares, since you're here as much for the *soigné* aura of the place as you are to eat, and this is a lovely spot to while away an evening.... *Tel 40 15 06 65; 41, rue de Lille, 75007; Métro Rue du Bac. Open noon–2:30pm, 7:30pm–2am daily. DC not accepted. $$$*

Le Vaudeville. Filled with stockbrokers at noon, this appealing pumpkin turns into a champagne flute as the night deepens. Who wouldn't love the nicotine-ambered faux marble mixed with the real stuff, the many mirrors inviting a wayward glance, the slightly catty art-deco decor, the speedy waiters, even the food? During the summer, it has a minuiscule but very pleasant terrace overlooking the empty square in front of the Paris stock exchange just across the street. Come here to sate almost any nocturnal appetite: for a big tray of freshly opened oysters mounted on a pile of crushed ice in the winter; for very good smoked salmon served with blinis and crème fraîche in the summer; with tasty foie gras, fish, and grills in between as fancy strikes you. Note that the house Riesling is better than harmless.... *Tel 40 20 04 62; 29, rue Vivienne; Métro Bourse. Open daily 11am–2am. $$*

Yvan-sur-Seine. Celebrity chef Yvan has a hit on his hands with this new late-night bistro on the banks of the Seine. To understand the mood here, imagine what the Love Boat would have been like if the Village People had climbed aboard. The snug dining room is done in wood paneling to resemble the interior of an old barge captain, and the Ritchie Family and other seventies disco greats dominate the soundtrack, much to the delight of a mostly male professional crowd that may be thinking back wistfully on younger, gamier moments in life. If the crowd's sometimes half gay, the overall mix is diverse and very friendly, and younger, too, as the night goes on. People chat easily between tables, and this isn't a bad place to come for news of the very latest in naughty after-hours pleasures in Paris. The good-value 138-franc prix fixe menu offers a starter, main course, and dessert, of which the stuffed eggplant appetizer, skirt steak with sautéed potatoes, and pear tart are delicious. Regulars love the grilled salmon with buttered cabbage on the à la carte menu.... *Tel 42 36 49 52; quai du Louvre, 75001; Métro Louvre. Reservations suggested. Daily noon–2:30pm, 8pm–4am. $$*

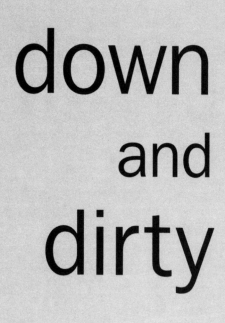

down
and
dirty

Babysitters... Two reputable agencies provide English-speaking babysitters (most often older women with some nanny experience, or former au pairs): **Home Service** (tel 42 82 05 04) and **Kid Service** (tel 47 66 00 52). Kid Service has been operating for 20 years and has a larger available pool of sitters. Both charge about 30 francs per hour (though rates vary depending on the number of kiddies to oversee) and require a three-hour minimum stay. Also check with your hotel concierge or front desk about sitters; they'll often have a few to recommend.

Buses... The RATP runs the 58 bus lines that crisscross the city. Transport above ground affords more sightseeing, though most of the buses run until 8:30pm only and cost twice as much as a Métro fare. The godsend alternative to the 8:30 closing time are ten **Noctambuses** that operate until 11pm, ferrying tourists to most of the major guide-book spots; you can spot them by the yellow and black shield with an image of an owl and a moon on the front of the bus. The bus station for the Noctambuses is Châtelet, at avenue Victoria, and all en-route Noctambuses must be flagged. Tickets are bought on board and the drivers can usually eke out English.

Car rental... If you are confining your visit to Paris, there really is no need to rent a car. Public transportation is reliable and cheap, and taxis can always be used in a pinch. Car rental in France is very expensive and parking in Paris is an urban nightmare to the nth degree. But if you must rent, try to book a car from home. One option is a fly/drive package that a travel agent can set up for you. In France, you won't need an international driver's license (unless you plan to rent a car for more than a year), and you'll see familiar car rental companies such as **Avis** (tel 46 10 60 60) and **Hertz** (tel 47 88 51 51). Both have branches in the Orly and Charles de Gaulle airports, in the train stations, and dotted about town. And both are on the pricier side. Two European companies that are reliable and lower-priced are **Europcar** (tel 30 43 82 82) and **EuroDollar** (tel 49 38 77 77). Petrol is pricey, too, so choose the smallest car available.

Chauffeurs... Why not a chauffeur-driven Mercedes for your big night on the town? It's so much more convenient than a taxi. All drivers of the **International Limousine** (tel 53 81 14 14) are English-speaking, too. You can also try **Prestige Limousines** (tel 42 50 81 81).

Credit card help... For lost or stolen credit cards or traveler's checks: **American Express** (tel 47 77 72 00) and **Visa/MasterCard** (tel 42 77 11 90).

Festivals and special events...

January: **Le Salon International de la Navigation de Plaisance** is one of the continent's largest boat shows, with a seemingly endless flotilla of *bateaux* (Parc des Expositions, Porte de Versailles; Métro Porte de Versailles). Supermodels, runways, haute couture, a jungle of photographers, and the hip buzz of the fashion world hold **Prêt-à-Porter** shows at the Parc des Expositions and at other citywide locales from mid-January to mid-February (Parc des Expositions, Porte de Versailles; Métro Porte de Versailles).

February: **18 Heures-18 Francs**. All films playing at selected theaters are 18 francs for the 6pm show.

March: Saint-Denis hosts the **Banlieue Bleues** jazz festival (tel 43 85 66 00); and the **Foire de Trône** amusement park is open from the end of the month through May (Métro Château de Vincennes).

April: More than 15,000 runners pound the Parisian pavement on the third weekend of the month for the **Paris Marathon** (tel 53 17 01 10). The race begins on the Champs-Elysées and wends past some of the city's most famous sites.

May: In Paris, the French Tennis Open is called the **Tournée Roland Garros**, after the stadium where it's held, and the Grand Slam tourney is one of the city's most popular annual spectator sports, with equal doses of rackets and posing (tel 47 43 48 00; Stade Roland Garros, 2, av. Gordon-Bennet, 75016). Antiques dealers converge in the seventh arrondissement's Carré Rive Gauche (an area bordered by quai Voltaire, rue de l'Université, rue des Saints-Pères, and rue du Bac) for five days at the end of the month called **Cinq Jours de l'Objet Extraordinaire** (tel 42 61 31 45).

June: **Festival St-Denis** is a series of choral concerts that runs through June and July. The emphasis is on "big," with choral works being performed at the Basilique St-Denis. At the monthlong **Festival du Marais**, the trendy neighborhood presents al fresco performances of jazz, classical music, theater, and fine arts in courtyards throughout the 'hood. **Festival Chopin** is an annual three-week piano festival featuring concerts *de Frédéric* of the mostly obscure variety (tel 45 01 20 50; Orangerie, Jardins de Bagatelle, 75016).

July: Holidays in France are called *jours fériés*, and **Bastille Day** on July 14 is one of the city's largest. The day begins with a parade down the Champs-Elysées. Shops, banks, and offices are closed, and it seems as if many Parisians spend the day lighting firecrackers and kissing strangers. Bars and restaurants often have special meals and parties. Though most Parisians bug out of town in summer, **Quartier d'Eté** (tel 44 83 64 40; held at Jardin du Luxembourg, Tuileries, the Sorbonne, and the Palais Royal), a monthlong festival from mid-July to mid-August, might be reason to stay. On the bill are classical and world-music performances, puppet shows, cabaret, theater, and circus acts. The **Tour de France** is bicycling's most grueling and famous race; it finishes in Paris in late July (for the actual date, call 49 35 69 00), as cyclists pedal down the Champs-Elysées after nearly 4,000 kilometers of cross-country cycling.

September: **Festival d'Automne à Paris** commissions and subsidizes new works in theater, music, and dance that are presented throughout the City of Lights from September to December (tel 42 96 12 27). Around mid-September is when the **Musique Baroque au Château de Versailles** kicks in. It runs through the middle of October and sponsors chamber music, opera, ballet, and theater productions performed in the regal surroundings of Versailles. The Baroque Music Center was founded in Versailles in 1987, and this festival is an annual celebration of the arts. **Journées du Patrimoine** (tel 44 61 20 00) is a holiday that is a sort of governmental open house, with historic and government buildings all over the country allowing visitors a peek inside. The most popular places (and the ones perennially with the longest lines) are Elysée Palace, the president's home; Hôtel Matignon, the prime minister's abode; Palais du Luxembourg, the Senate building; and the Palais Royal.

October: In the first week of October, the horsey set and wannabes attend the **Prix de l'Arc de Triomphe** (tel 49 10 20 30), one of European horse racing's top flat races.

November: **Armistice Day** is celebrated on November 11 with a military parade that marches from the Arc de Triomphe to the Hôtel des Invalides.

December: **Fête de Saint-Sylvestre**, known in the States as New Year's Eve, is the citywide love fest held near the midnight hour. Huge Times Square-esque crowds converge at the Arc de Triomphe, and the Champs-Elysées

PARIS 〰 DOWN AND DIRTY

becomes shoulder to shoulder with revelers kissing, drinking champagne, and shouting, *Bonne Année.*

Finding your way... For maps, brochures, and paperwork about the city's public transportation system (the city's 13 métro lines and the 58 citywide bus lines), the two offices of **Services Touristiques de la RATP** will help (tel 40 46 42 12; 53 bis, quai des Grands-Augustins, 75006; Métro Saint-Michel; or tel 43 46 14 14; place de la Madeleine, 75008; Métro Madeleine.)

Gay and lesbian resources... The gay and lesbian bible of sorts is the annually updated *Guide Gai,* a compendium of gay and lesbian clubs, hotels, bars, restaurants, and services. *Lesbia* is a monthly magazine geared toward lesbians; the magazine has a healthy section of listings for organizations and services, as well as a steamy personals section. **Les Mots à la Bouche** is the city's most well-known gay and lesbian bookstore (tel 42 78 88 30; 6, rue St-Croix-de-la Bretonnerie, 75004). Inside, there is a bulletin board, a friendly crowd, and a mind-blowing selection of gay and lesbian-oriented literature.

Libraries... The city is awash in libraries, though the two that are most user-friendly and amenable to English speakers are **The American Library** (tel 45 51 46 82; 10, rue du Général Camou, 75007; Métro Alma-Marceau) and **Bibliothèque Publique Information** (tel 44 78 12 33; Centre Pompidou, place Georges-Pompidou, 75004; Métro Rambuteau). The American Library charges a reading fee of about $10 an hour; the Pompidou library is stocked more fully with CDs, videos, books, and a thorough database system. It's also open until 10pm most nights.

Magazines... Two of the city's magazines are best known for their entertainment listings of theater, movies, exhibits, concerts, restaurants, and clubs: *Pariscope* and *L'Officiel des Spectacles.* Both are weeklies and available on Wednesdays at kiosks and in city bookstores. *7 à Paris* also lists musical events in town, including classical concerts. *Le Figaro,* a daily newspaper published in French, also has a listings section on Wednesdays that is easy enough to follow, even for those who *parlez* only tourist French. *Boulevard* is an English bimonthly, also available at newsstands, that is a source for reviews, trends, gossip, and star sightings.

Mail... The **main post office** in Paris, where you can mail letters, and send faxes and telegrams, is open 24 hours a day (tel 40 28 20 00; 52, rue du Louvre, 75001; Métro Les Halles).

Medical advice... For free legal and medical advice over the phone, Monday through Friday from 10am to 9pm, you can call **SOS Viol** (tel 05 05 95 95), a rape crisis line that parcels out a whole range of emergency advice in French and English. For a 24-hour doctor, call **SOS Médicin** (tel 43 37 77 77). An English-language crisis line, **SOS Help** (tel 47 23 80 80) is open daily until 11pm. Two local hospitals, **American Hospital** (tel 46 41 25 25; 63, bd. Victor Hugo Métro Pont de Lavallois Bécon) and British Hospital (tel 47 58 13 12; 3, rue Barbés; Métro Barbès-Rochechouart), have English-language doctors and staff. Both also have emergency rooms. Keep in mind that the fire department, or *Pompiers,* has its own ambulances and is often faster in arriving at the scene of an accident than hospital ambulances (tel 18).

Métro... The Paris subway is called **the Métro** (for info call 43 46 14 14), 13 lines operated by the RATP, Paris's mother transport company. The Métro is the fastest, cheapest, and often most convenient way to navigate the city. That's the good news. The bad news is that the Métro stops running at 1am. Dozens of Métro stations are sprinkled throughout the city; you'll recognize the large, encircled M used to identify the stations. At all Métro exits you'll find neighborhood maps, and inside the stations and the subway cars you'll see Métro maps. Métro tickets are sold in each station and are run through slots in turnstiles similar to the token-taking ones in New York City. The big difference between the New York and Paris subways: passengers need to remember to hang on to their tickets for the duration of the ride. Transit police troll the cars from time to time and will levy a fine on the spot if you don't have your validated ticket. If you're caught empty-handed, feign tourist ignorance; it's worth a try.

Money matters... Though banks offer the best exchange rates, they close early. Independent, nonbank exchange offices (*bureaux de change*) may hit you with lousier exchange rates, but they don't charge commissions, and their hours are longer; those in all the main train stations and a few near major tourist attractions are open until 9pm. Some names to look for are **CCF**, **Europullman**, **Société Financière de Change**, and **Barlor**. Also, such banking networks as Plus and Cirrus allow you to use your cash card at ATMs in Paris.

Parking... Parking in Paris is akin to a having migraine. If you dare to park in illegal zones (those marked *Parking*

Interdit or *Stationnement Interdit*), you'll either be towed or clamped with a boot by traffic police with an almost special brand of malice. If your car is towed, head to the nearest *Commisariat de Police* (police station). If you go the legal route, scour for a parking space marked with a *P* or a *Parking Payant* sign. Step Two is to fork over your franc coins into the nearby parking machine, called a *horodateur*. The machine spits out a ticket that you then display on your windshield. Parking is free on weekends, public holidays, and during the month of August (maybe because during August the city is ceded to tourists who don't know about this and plunk their money into the machines anyway).

Pharmacies... The **Pharmacie Européenne** (tel 48 74 65 18; 6, place de Clichy, 75017; Métro Place de Clichy) and the **Derhy-Pharmacie des Champs** (tel 45 62 02 41; 84, av. des Champs-Elysées, 75008; Métro George-V) are open 24 hours daily.

Radio... *Quel dommage,* but there are no English-language radio stations in Paris, even though you will hear British and American songs interspersed with French hits. The kind of station you want to have as background music is **FIP** (105.1 FM); it is without commercials and plays classical music and jazz announced by breathy shejays. Another station that would be called alternative in the States is **Radio Nova** (101.5 FM), which mixes hip-hop, acid jazz, funk, and reggae. For rock 'n' roll fans there is **RFM** (103.9 FM) and **Skyrock** (96 FM). **France-Info** (105.5 FM) is a 24-hour news station in French. **Radio Montmartre** (102.7 FM) is a French oldies station (attention Piaf, Brel, and Trenet fans), and classical music lovers can turn to **Radio Classique** (101.1 FM).

Safety... Though Paris crawls with more than 2 million people, street crime—muggings, purse snatching, pickpocketing, female harassment—is much more infrequent than in the States. But still, use big-city caution when you're out at night. Always keep cash on hand, because credit cards aren't accepted as readily as they are stateside, and cabs do not take traveler's checks or plastic. It's also best to avoid RER train stations at night. Those are the lines that service the burbs, and groups of drunken teenagers have been known to congregate, looking for trouble. To reach the police, dial 17 on phones. In case of emergencies while riding the Métro, cars are outfitted with yellow telephones marked *chef de station.*

Scooters... The best organized scooter rental agency in Paris, **Agence Contact Location** (tel 47 66 19 19; 10 bis, avenue de la Grande Armée, 75017; Métro Charles-de-Gaulle-Etoile; closed Sun), offers a range of different two-wheelers, including motorcycles. Prices depend upon the power of your bike. A 50cc motor scooter costs 230F a day and 850F a week, plus a hefty deposit on your credit card, insurance included. A valid driver's license is required.

Sports hotline... **Allô Sports** (tel 42 76 54 54) gives dates, ticket information, and a calendar of sports events in the Paris area.

Taxis... If you eschew sharing transportation with the plebeian masses, you can always opt for a taxi. Though more than 10,000 cabs troll the City of Lights, there's always a dearth on Friday and Saturday nights. You've got two ways to get a cab: flag one on the street or join the line at a taxi stand, called a rank. You can find ranks at all hospitals, train stations, airports, main Métro stations, and busy intersections. Rates are higher for nighttime cab rides (you'll see Rate B show up on the meter). There are also extra charges if you get a taxi at a train station or airport, if your luggage weighs more than 5 kilograms, if there's a fourth person or if you have an animal with you. Radio-dispatched taxis are available from **Alpha-Taxis** (tel 45 85 85 85), **Artaxi** (tel 42 41 50 50), and **G7 Radio** (tel 47 39 47 39).

Tickets... Aside from going directly to box offices (which are usually open from 11am–7pm), the easiest way to get concert tickets is to stop by an **FNAC** (main branch: tel 40 41 40 00; Forum des Halles, 1, rue Pierre-Lescot; Métro Les Halles). Each branch of this chain (and there are at least a dozen sprinkled throughout the city) of book and electronic stores has a ticket counter where current and advance gigs are listed and sold; the staff often speaks English, too. Another source is the **Virgin Megastore** (tel 40 74 06 48; 52–60, av. Champs-Elysées; Métro Champs-Elysées-Clemenceau) for last-minute, cheapo tickets. For half-price tickets to current theater, sold on the day of the performance, try the two branches of **Kiosque Théâtre** (tel 42 65 52 17; place de la Madeleine; Métro Madeleine; open 12:30–8pm daily and in the RER station of Châtelet-Les Halles; Métro Châtelet-Les Halles RER; open 12:30–6pm Tuesday through Saturday). Be aware, though, that a ticket marked *sans visibilité* means you'll be lucky if you get to see the stage; you'll have a partial view, if any. If all else fails, buy a couple of *sv* tickets, and palm the usher at the show a few francs to steer you toward no-show seats.

Tourist offices... There are seven tourist offices in the city: one at each of the five main SNCF train stations, one on the Champs-Elysées, and one near the Eiffel Tower. The **Office du Tourisme et des Congrès de Paris** has two branches; the main office (tel 49 52 53 56/English-speaking help, 49 52 53 54/French; 127, av. des Champs-Elysées, 75008; Métro Champs-Elysées-Clemenceau; open until 8pm nightly) and the Eiffel Tower office (tel 45 50 34 36; Champ de Mars, 75007; Métro Ecole Militaire; open nightly until 6pm), and enough maps, leaflets, and brochures to paper the Arc de Triomphe. Both offices have a recorded telephone-information service that provides info about concerts and transportation. There are also tourist offices in five train stations: Gare d'Austerlitz (tel 45 84 91 70; Métro Gare D'Austerlitz), Gare de l'Est (tel 46 07 17 73; Métro Gare de l'Est), Gare de Lyon (tel 43 43 33 24; Métro Gare de Lyon), Gare Montparnasse (tel 43 22 19 19; Métro Montparnasse-Bienvenüe), and Gare du Nord (tel 45 26 94 82; Métro Gare du Nord). All five are open until 9pm.

Travelers with disabilities... Paris does not make it easy for the disabled traveler: All the Métro stations have stairs only, and only one of the city's 58 bus lines has access for wheelchairs (it's line 20, which runs between Gare de Lyon and Gare Saint-Lazare). The good news is that the taxis in town are required to help with wheelchairs (though the bad news is that some won't stop for disabled passengers). The city sidewalks all have ramps and curb-cuts on corners. Many of the city's hotels have elevators, but they're tiny and often unable to accommodate the width of a wheelchair. Hotel bathrooms are also a problem—often too small for wheelchair access. The **Paris Tourism Office** (tel 49 52 53 54; 127 av. des Champs-Elysées, 75008; open daily until 8pm) has information about hotels, museums, monuments, and transportation that is accessible. If you need an escort while in the city, **Les Compagnons de Voyage** (tel 45 83 67 77; 7, bd. de l'Hôpital, 75013; open daily until 5pm) provides escorts and tour guides for a fee, though their availability at night is limited.

Now Save Money On All Your Travels By Joining
FROMMER'S™ TRAVEL BOOK CLUB
The World's Best Travel Guides
At Membership Prices!

Frommer's Travel Book Club is your ticket to successful travel! Open up a world of travel information and simplify your travel planning when you join ranks with thousands of value-conscious travelers who are members of the Frommer's *Travel Book Club.* Join today and you'll be entitled to all the privileges that come from belonging to the club that offers you travel guides for less to more than 100 destinations worldwide. **Annual membership is only $25.00 (U.S.) or $35.00 (Canada/Foreign).**

The Advantages of Membership:

1. Your choice of **three free** books (any **two** Frommer's Comprehensive Guides, Frommer's $-A-Day Guides, Frommer's Walking Tours or Frommer's Family Guides—plus **one** Frommer's City Guide, Frommer's City $-A-Day Guide or Frommer's Touring Guide).

2. Your own subscription to the **TRIPS & TRAVEL** quarterly newsletter.

3. You're entitled to a **30% discount** on your order of any additional books offered by the club.

4. You're offered (at a small additional fee) our **Domestic Trip-Routing Kits.**

Our **Trips & Travel** quarterly newsletter offers practical information on the best buys in travel, the "hottest" vacation spots, the latest travel trends, world-class events and much, much more.

Our **Domestic Trip-Routing Kits** are available for any North American destination. We'll send you a detailed map highlighting the best route to take to your destination—you can request direct or scenic routes.

Here's all you have to do to join:
Send in your membership fee of $25.00 ($35.00 Canada/Foreign) with your name and address on the form below along with your selections as part of your membership package to the address listed below. Remember to check off your three free books.

If you would like to order additional books, please select the books you would like and send a check for the total amount (please add sales tax in the states noted below), plus $2.00 per book for shipping and handling ($3.00 Canada/Foreign) to the address listed below.

FROMMER'S TRAVEL BOOK CLUB
P.O. Box 473
Mt. Morris, IL 61054-0473
(815) 734-1104

[ ] **YES!** I want to take advantage of this opportunity to join Frommer's Travel Book Club.

[ ] My check is enclosed. Dollar amount enclosed_____*
(all payments in U.S. funds only)

Name _____

Address _____

City _____ State _____ Zip _____

Phone ( ) _____ (In case we have a question regarding your order).

All orders must be prepaid.

To ensure that all orders are processed efficiently, please apply sales tax in the following areas: CA, CT, FL, IL, IN, NJ, NY, PA, TN, WA and CANADA.

*With membership, shipping & handling will be paid by Frommer's Travel Book Club for the three FREE books you select as part of your membership. Please add $2.00 per book for shipping & handling for any additional books purchased ($3.00 Canada/Foreign).

Allow 4-6 weeks for delivery for all items. Prices of books, membership fee, and publication dates are subject to change without notice. All orders are subject to acceptance and availability.

Please send me the books checked below:

FROMMER'S COMPREHENSIVE GUIDES

*(Guides listing facilities from budget to deluxe,
with emphasis on the medium-priced)*

	Retail Price	Code		Retail Price	Code
☐ Acapulco/Ixtapa/Taxco, 2nd Edition	$13.95	C157	☐ Jamaica/Barbados, 2nd Edition	$15.00	C149
☐ Alaska '94-'95	$17.00	C131	☐ Japan '94-'95	$19.00	C144
☐ Arizona '95 (Avail. 3/95)	$14.95	C166	☐ Maui, 1st Edition	$14.00	C153
☐ Australia '94'-'95	$18.00	C147	☐ Nepal, 2nd Edition	$18.00	C126
☐ Austria, 6th Edition	$16.95	C162	☐ New England '95	$16.95	C165
☐ Bahamas '94-'95	$17.00	C121	☐ New Mexico, 3rd Edition (Avail. 3/95)	$14.95	C167
☐ Belgium/Holland/ Luxembourg '93-'94	$18.00	C106	☐ New York State '94-'95	$19.00	C133
☐ Bermuda '94-'95	$15.00	C122	☐ Northwest, 5th Edition	$17.00	C140
☐ Brazil, 3rd Edition	$20.00	C111	☐ Portugal '94-'95	$17.00	C141
☐ California '95	$16.95	C164	☐ Puerto Rico '95-'96	$14.00	C151
☐ Canada '94-'95	$19.00	C145	☐ Puerto Vallarta/ Manzanillo/Guadalajara '94-'95	$14.00	C135
☐ Caribbean '95	$18.00	C148			
☐ Carolinas/Georgia, 2nd Edition	$17.00	C128			
☐ Colorado, 2nd Edition	$16.00	C143	☐ Scandinavia, 16th Edition (Avail. 3/95)	$19.95	C169
☐ Costa Rica '95	$13.95	C161	☐ Scotland '94-'95	$17.00	C146
☐ Cruises '95-'96	$19.00	C150	☐ South Pacific '94-'95	$20.00	C138
☐ Delaware/Maryland '94-'95	$15.00	C136	☐ Spain, 16th Edition	$16.95	C163
☐ England '95	$17.95	C159	☐ Switzerland/ Liechtenstein '94-'95	$19.00	C139
☐ Florida '95	$18.00	C152	☐ Thailand, 2nd Edition	$17.95	C154
☐ France '94-'95	$20.00	C132	☐ U.S.A., 4th Edition	$18.95	C156
☐ Germany '95	$18.95	C158	☐ Virgin Islands '94-'95	$13.00	C127
☐ Ireland, 1st Edition (Avail. 3/95)	$16.95	C168	☐ Virginia '94-'95	$14.00	C142
☐ Italy '95	$18.95	C160	☐ Yucatan, 2nd Edition	$13.95	C155

FROMMER'S $-A-DAY GUIDES

(Guides to low-cost tourist accommodations and facilities)

	Retail Price	Code		Retail Price	Code
☐ Australia on $45 '95-'96	$18.00	D122	☐ Israel on $45, 15th Edition	$16.95	D130
☐ Costa Rica/Guatemala/ Belize on $35, 3rd Edition	$15.95	D126	☐ Mexico on $45 '95	$16.95	D125
			☐ New York on $70 '94-'95	$16.00	D121
☐ Eastern Europe on $30, 5th Edition	$16.95	D129	☐ New Zealand on $45 '93-'94	$18.00	D103
☐ England on $60 '95	$17.95	D128			
☐ Europe on $50 '95	$17.95	D127	☐ South America on $40, 16th Edition	$18.95	D123
☐ Greece on $45 '93-'94	$19.00	D100			
☐ Hawaii on $75 '95	$16.95	D124	☐ Washington, D.C. on $50 '94-'95	$17.00	D120
☐ Ireland on $45 '94-'95	$17.00	D118			